SPANISH-LANGUAGE RADIO IN THE
SOUTHWESTERN UNITED STATES

MONOGRAPH NUMBER 5
CENTER FOR MEXICAN AMERICAN STUDIES
THE UNIVERSITY OF TEXAS AT AUSTIN

SPANISH-LANGUAGE RADIO IN THE SOUTHWESTERN UNITED STATES

By

FÉLIX F. GUTIÉRREZ
School of Journalism
University of Southern California

JORGE REINA SCHEMENT
Department of Radio/Television/Film
The University of Texas at Austin

CENTER FOR MEXICAN AMERICAN STUDIES
THE UNIVERSITY OF TEXAS AT AUSTIN

This book is dedicated to our families, without whose love, support, encouragement and sacrifice we would not have been able to even dream of writing a book. Therefore, we dedicate this book to our parents, Rebecca and the late Félix Gutiérrez and Berta and Vincent Schement; to our wives, María Elena and Susan Heck; and to our children, Elena, Anita, and Alicia Gutiérrez and Elisa Schement-Heck.

Contents

Preface

This monograph is the end result of a five-year study of Spanish-language radio conducted as graduate students at Stanford University and, later, as faculty members at California State University, Northridge and the University of Texas at Austin. But, institutional affiliations aside, the motivation for this effort was our interest as Chicanos in studying the forces that have shaped and developed a communication medium that is in a position to exert growing influence over our community.

Our effort has had the continuing support and encouragement of a number of individuals and organizations. The most important of these has been the interest of our families: parents, wives, and children. To them we owe a continuing debt of gratitude. Special thanks should also go to the faculty members who worked with the project when we were graduate students: Jerry Porras, Emile McAnany, William Rivers, Everett Rogers and Lyle Nelson at Stanford University and Carlos Muñoz, now at the University of California at Berkeley. Our efforts were also subsequently encouraged and commented upon at Stanford by: Armando Valdez, Ernesto Ballesteros, David Martínez, Mario Evangelista, Norma Sosa, Carlota Jaramillo, Homero Galicia, Guillermo Flores, Ramón Chacón, Margie Hernández, Isabel Valdieviezo, Cecilia Burciaga and Marc Porat. Without the continued interest and support on their part this project could not have been successfully completed. Two others who have given willingly and unselfishly in working closely with us in our studies of Spanish-language radio are Nicholas Valenzuela of Stanford University and Loy Alonzo Singleton of the University of Texas at Austin. We hope they will continue their research in this area, for there is much remaining to be learned and they can contribute substantially to the knowledge in this field.

We must also thank those persons working in the Spanish-language radio stations across the Southwest for their interest in our project, their suggestions, and their cooperation with our research efforts. From them we gained many valuable insights and understandings about the development and operation of Spanish-language radio. Our study is stronger for their contributions.

Financial support and in-kind contributions to this work over the years came from a number of sources interested in the project. They include: The Chicano Fellows and the Office of the Assistant to the President at Stanford University; The Department of Journalism at California State University, Northridge; The Department of Radio/Television/Film and Center for Mexican American Studies at the University of Texas at Austin; the Graduate Fellowships for Mexican Americans of The Ford Foundation; the Post-Doctoral Fellowships Program of the National Chicano Council on Higher Education; the California La Raza Media Coalition; and our families.

Finally, a very special thanks must go to Efraím P. Armendáriz and Américo Paredes of the Center for Mexican American Studies, Gilberto Cárdenas of the Department of Sociology, and Timothy Meyer of the Department of Radio/Television/Film at the University of Texas at Austin. Their encouragement of our hopes for publication and their comments and suggestions on the manuscript contributed greatly to the successful completion of the project.

SPANISH-LANGUAGE RADIO IN THE
SOUTHWESTERN UNITED STATES

CHAPTER I

The Surprising Growth of Spanish-language Radio

Every morning millions of persons across the United States wake up and turn to their radio for music, news and traffic reports. During the day they listen to radio as they drive to work, go about their daily tasks, and make their way home. For them radio is a "constant companion," the communication medium that follows them wherever they go.

Radio is also the "constant companion" to millions of Spanish-speaking Latinos in the United States. Over the past 50 years Spanish-language radio has grown from an occasional voice heard on isolated stations in the Southwest and on big city multilingual stations to a multimillion dollar segment of the broadcast industry. In the Southwest big city stations such as San Antonio's KCOR, Albuquerque's KABQ, Phoenix's KIFN, Denver's KBNO and Los Angeles' KALI attract large shares of the listeners in their communities.

For many Spanish-speaking listeners who have limited ability to use English-language media, Spanish-language radio is a primary source of news, entertainment, and advertising. But as Spanish-language radio addresses the needs of its audience it also serves the economic interests of its owners and advertisers. For these reasons Spanish-language radio has experienced tremendous growth in the 1970s; and even more growth can be projected to keep pace with the anticipated growth of U.S. Latinos over the next generation.

Latinos in the United States

Latinos are the nation's fastest growing racial population group and their numbers are expected to grow at an even faster rate as the U.S. reaches the 21st century.[1] According to the U.S. Bureau of the Census, which admits it has not accurately enumerated the group, there are

3

about 12 million Latinos in the country. With an additional 3.1 million Puerto Rican citizens and an estimated six to eight million undocumented immigrants (the government's most conservative figures) the total easily tops 20 million. Between 1970 and 1975 the nation's Latino population grew by 20 percent, five times the national average, and steady growth is expected to continue for several reasons.

One reason is that because of a younger median age than the national average (20.9 years for Latinos and 28.9 years for the U.S. overall), the Latino population will be entering its most productive child birth years at a time when other sectors are passing out of it. Another factor is the larger anticipated family sizes of Latinos. Continued immigration from Latin America is a third factor. To these are added the political factors of statehood for Puerto Rico and some form of amnesty for undocumented residents. Even without the political factors Latinos will surpass Blacks for the dubious honor of being the nation's largest minority group sometime in the future. Demographers predict this will happen sometime early in the next century. But some government officials predict it could occur as early as 1990.

Long stereotyped as a regional or rural group found in large numbers only in the Southwest and a few urban areas such as Miami, Latinos are actually a nationally dispersed group with large population centers in the Midwest and Northeast. The U.S. city with the largest Latino population is New York City. The states of New York, New Jersey and Illinois each have more Latinos than either Arizona, Colorado or New Mexico. In addition, New York, Chicago, Philadelphia, and Washington, D.C. rank among the nation's top 25 Latino population centers. About 85 percent of all Latinos live in urban areas and Latinos have a lower percentage of their work force employed as farm labor than the U.S. labor force overall.

But large numbers and urban representation have not resulted in a better life for U.S. Latinos. Most still face a stiff uphill battle in working to improve their lives and communities. Median family income for Latinos is 25 percent below the U.S. average and nearly one-fourth of all Latinos live in poverty. Other social indicators such as education, housing, health, employment, and political representation consistently show Latinos far below national norms.

Latinos and Broadcasting

But individual poverty can be measured as collective wealth by advertisers, marketing strategists, and media managers eager to penetrate this growing segment of the U.S. population. Since audience and marketing studies show that Latinos, like other low income populations, tend to be heavy users of broadcast media and prefer Spanish-language broadcasting where it is available, the rise in the population has been accompanied by a steep growth in Spanish-language broadcasting in the past 15 years.

According to figures from the *Broadcasting Yearbook* the growth of Spanish-language broadcasting in the 1970s has been spectacular. For instance, the 1973 *Yearbook* listed about 250 radio stations airing Spanish-language programs in the United States.[2] By 1978 the *Yearbook* listed over 600 stations (more than double the 1973 figure), about 100 of those featuring Spanish as their primary format.[3] The *1978 Broadcasting Yearbook* also listed 21 television stations with primary programming in Spanish,[4] a listing the 1973 *Yearbook* did not even carry.

Advertisers ride the Spanish-language airwaves to cash in on the estimated $31 billion annual consumer market that Latinos represent in the United States. The advertisers have sharply stepped up their advertising efforts to reach Latinos and are becoming increasingly sophisticated in their advertising strategies to penetrate and persuade the Spanish-speaking audience.[5] A 1972 marketing magazine estimated advertisers were then spending $40 million on Spanish-language media.[6] By 1977 *Television/Radio Age* put the figure between $60 million and $70 million, but reported "some estimates are much higher."[7] These estimates run to $125 million a year, with $90 million of that spent on Spanish-language broadcasting.[8]

The Evolution of Spanish-language Radio

Times have not always been so affluent for Spanish-language radio, especially in the 1920s and 1930s when radio stations began selling blocks of time for Spanish-language programs to Latino brokers. The brokers, sometimes negotiating with the station through agents, paid the stations a flat rate for the airtime, sold advertisements to local businesses, and programmed the broadcasts themselves. The difference between what they took in from advertising and paid to the station for the airtime was their profit.[9]

From the beginning the "business behind the box" was economic competition. Stations would sometimes sell to foreign language brokers only time slots that were unprofitable for English-language programs, such as early mornings or weekends. In other cases, marginally profitable stations with restrictions on broadcast hours or power would turn to foreign-language programming when the English-language market proved too competitive. And, from the start, the motivation behind the message was delivery of commercial advertising to the non-English speaking audience. One pioneer foreign language broadcaster described how foreign-language programming developed on the East Coast:

> Such (foreign language) programs took shape in the early thirties when business was slack and competition between the smaller stations keen. They discovered that the emotional impact of an advertising message delivered in a listener's first-learned language and suggestively enfolded in a program of music or drama evoking the most nostalgic memories of a listener's far-away birthplace was infinitely greater than the same message in English. They also made the sinister discovery that nationality—even in America—has competitive value: Poles will more readily buy from Poles, Italians from Italians and so on.[10]

In the Southwestern United States, where Chicanos constituted a large part of the population, radio stations sold time to Spanish-language brokers, many of them with previous experience in Mexican broadcasting or theater. One of the first successful brokers was a Sr. Lozano, who began a brokered program on San Antonio's KONO in 1928, just four years after the first radio station opened in the city.[11] Rodolfo Hoyos, who was on the air in Los Angeles from 1932 through 1967, recalled in a 1974 interview that his early programs were a mixture of live music, poetry, drama and discussion. He described his early programs as a broker and the subsequent change to recorded programs:

> We would present artists, I would sing and have many artists. There were groups of singers. We would put radio dramas with recognized artists, such as Romualdo Tirado and José Peña Pepén, who were artists here in the theater. I would put dramas on the radio, first live and then using records. I began to use records and it became easier for us and less expensive. Before it cost us to pay the artists, although we paid them relatively little, but it cost money. Of course, if I presented an artist that was paid five or 10 dollars a day, in a week [it amounted to] 60 dollars and one thing and another. Well that was plenty for us. So we began to play records.[12]

In the early days Hoyos paid the station $180 a week for a daily show of one hour. He also sold advertising in addition to producing the show. Advertisers paid from $50 to $60 a month for a daily announcement on the program. Most of the advertising came from companies doing business primarily with "la colonia Mexicana" and Hoyos spent much of his day visiting local businesses selling advertising and making collections.

Based on the brokerage system, Spanish-language radio continued to grow in the Southwest and by the late 1930s a number of stations were airing Spanish programs. Some of the programs were of short duration, while others had longer runs as daily programs. In 1939 the International Broadcasting Company, based in El Paso, began to produce and sell Spanish-language programs to different stations in the United States. The firm was headed by Lester Farber and featured Mexican radio personalities José Samaniego and Fernando Navarro.[13]

A 1941 content analysis of foreign-language broadcasting in the United States by Arnheim and Bayne included Spanish-language programs in New York, Arizona, Texas and California. The researchers estimated that 264 hours Spanish were being broadcast each week by United States broadcasters.[14] They also found that many Spanish-language "programs" were actually sustaining broadcasts filled in as background between commercials. Of the Spanish-language broadcasts only 17.5% were sponsored, the rest airing spot advertisements between programming. Although this is currently the way most radio programming is now operated, in the 1940s advertisers preferred to sponsor specific programs. Thus, it would appear that Spanish-language programmers were ahead of what was to later become the dominant method of broadcast advertising.

The content analysis also showed the following breakdowns in Spanish-language program content: Musical, 88.1%; news, 4.2%; drama, 2.6%; talks, 3.1%; other, 2%. Spanish-language broadcasters devoted more time to music than the other foreign language broadcasters surveyed, again preceding a trend that would come to dominate most radio stations. In another interesting set of findings the researchers found that, when compared with other foreign-language broadcasters, there was greater listening by young Chicanos to Spanish-language radio and found that Spanish-language stations played more "national" (or Mexican) records than the others. The news on Spanish-language broadcasts was described as 80% from foreign countries, with heavy attention to news from Mexico.

In terms of advertising, the heaviest single category of advertisers on Spanish-language broadcasts was medicines, with movies and foods close by. Other strong advertisers included women's clothes, furniture, men's clothes, and beverages. Spanish programs were found to have the lowest advertising density of any foreign language programs, with an average of just over five sponsors announced each hour. Spanish advertisements were also found to be more highly concentrated around products and commercial services than other foreign-language broad-

7

casters, who often advertised entertainment, meetings, and travel abroad.

In terms of advertising appeal, Arnheim and Bayne found that nationalistic appeals were strong on all stations. These included advertising of national products, advertising referring to the home country, mentioning stores employing Spanish-speaking personnel, making an appeal on national obligations and making an appeal on unity of the group. Examples of nationalistic appeals directed to Chicanos included the following:

> If you want to wear typical Mexican costumes on Charro Days (fiesta) be sure and buy them at Paredes Dry Goods Store in Matamoros. Mexicans should wear typical Mexican costumes.

> They speak perfect Spanish at the T. Automobile Company. Many Mexicans have bought cars at the T. Automobile Company and have been highly satisfied.

> Go where the majority of employees is Mexican and where your own language is spoken.

> A Mexican will always get better values from another Mexican. So get your Chevrolet from a Mexican agent at the Central Chevrolet Company.[15]

Other popular announcements on Spanish-language programs were notices of community activities such as dances, church gatherings, clubs, and letter exchanges. Along these lines, a great number of stations apparently aired musical dedications on birthdays, anniversaries, and other special occasions sponsored by friends and relatives. Public service announcements on Spanish-language stations appeared to concentrate on facilitating interaction with Anglos and socialization to life in the United States. Arnheim and Bayne wrote:

> Mexicans were advised to register with the immigration authorities and, repeatedly on one program, "to keep out of trouble." Announcements praising American citizenship as an attractive thing to Mexicans were absent, although ways and means were presented in several announcements for those who were interested. In connection with such an appeal for Americanization, Mexicans were invited to go to night school, to pay income tax, etc.[16]

These authors, writing in a period when the United States was approaching World War II, perceived a duality in foreign language radio that they saw as both a threat and asset to the United States. On one hand foreign-language broadcasts appeared to reinforce identification with the language, customs, happenings, and culture of countries outside the United States and thus could be seen as a threat to national unity. On the other, the stations could be used in the socialization of foreign-language groups to reach them with messages which would infuse "the American view" into their lives.

A year later, after the war broke out, foreign language broadcasting became a hot issue when some government officials accused broadcasters of not exercising adequate control over the brokers and allowing programs that were potentially subversive. Although Spanish-language broadcasters were not directly accused, they became bound by unusually restrictive regulations by the U.S. Office of Censorship. The wartime foreign-language regulations were more stringent than those imposed on English-language broadcasters,[17] a double standard of federal broadcast regulation that continued in the post-war period and into the 1970s.[18] At the outset of the war it was reported that 200 broadcasters were offering foreign-language programs, many of them offering different languages in succession in what became known as block programming. Spanish was heard on 58 of the 200 stations and was the third most popular foreign-language aired, behind Polish and Italian.[19]

During the war San Antonio broker Raul Cortez applied to the Federal Communications Commission (FCC) for a license to operate a full time Spanish-language station, offering as part of the rationale the need to mobilize Chicanos behind the war effort.[20]

The station, KCOR, did not go on the air until 1946, but was apparently the first full time Spanish-language station owned and operated by a Chicano. Other expansion came after the war when the AM broadcast range was extended to 1600 khz and, according to a veteran Spanish-language radio manager, broadcasters on the outlying frequencies programmed to minorities who would turn the dial farther to get the specialized programming they preferred.[21] Hoyos recalled that after the war the station managements began to notice the brokers were tapping an audience they had not seen before and began to devote more time to Spanish-language programming because it was so profitable. As Spanish-language radio became big business some former brokers, like Denver's Paco Sanchez[22] and San Antonio's Cortez,[23] became owners of full time Spanish-language stations during the 1940s and 1950s. But most, like Los Angeles' Hoyos, were made employees of the stations they had formerly bought time from and were paid a salary and commission for the advertising they sold or aired.

9

The arrangements varied from station to station and region to region during the 1950s, as Spanish-language radio was in transition. On some stations all announcers were made employees. On others time was still sold to brokers and staff announcers filled in during sustaining time. On still others the broker system continued. The period continued the heyday of "personality radio" on the Spanish-language stations. The air personalities, whether brokers or employees, had a financial stake in the ability of their program to attract an audience for advertisers. Most continued to select their own music and deliver commercials themselves. Listener loyalty was toward the on-the-air personality, not the station itself. In many Southwestern communities radio personalities became an influential entrepreneurial class, passing along not only music, but advertisements and advice on current affairs. The announcers also supplemented their income by charging listeners for "dedicaciones" or songs played on anniversaries, birthdays and other special occasions. They often added their personal endorsements to products and businesses advertised and, in the words of one former announcer, "it was hard to know where the commercial left off and the program began."

The transitional period also witnessed the growing strength of Spanish-lanuguage radio within the broadcast industry. Surveys in 1956 and 1960 revealed that Spanish-language radio alone accounted for two-thirds of all the foreign language broadcasting in the United States.[24] It was during the 1960s that the broadcast trade press and researchers began to pay greater attention to the impact of Spanish-language radio on the broadcast industry and the Latino community. Broadcast publications began running wrapups on Spanish-language broadcasting and its audience.[25] Scholars began examining the medium and its interaction with Chicanos more carefully. These scholarly studies from the 1960s provide provocative questions about the dual role of Spanish-language radio in the Chicano community.

For example, Graham in a 1962 article on Denver's KFSC stressed the "Mexicanness" of the station and those who operated it, but also alluded to the socializing influence of Spanish-language radio:

> Although primarily a commercial undertaking, it is to a considerable degree the mouthpiece of a group with an awakening political awareness. It reflects their yearnings for greater political influence and increased social status, not however, as a minority group, but as American citizens. Possibly, this Spanish-speaking radio station will continue to be an important vehicle of expression for

them even if they completely adopt English. Listening to these broadcasts, one realizes that the station, while selling goods and services in Spanish, is also projecting American life in a language most acceptable to its listeners. It is, so to speak, an agent of acculturation even though this was never its conscious purpose.[26]

By 1966 Christian and Christian reported there were more than 300 radio stations broadcasting Spanish in the United States, two-thirds of them in the Southwest, and called the stations "the one and only force which is now promoting (use of) Spanish."[27] Most of the programming consisted of music and novelas (soap operas), with lesser amounts of poetry and news. Like Graham, Christian and Christian noted the utility of Spanish-language radio as a potential link between Anglos and Chicanos. They wrote:

> Program managers of Spanish stations and Spanish programs would like to see greater interest in and use of the Spanish language because this would increase their potential market. They comprise the largest single groups of leaders of the Spanish-speaking who are directly interested in the language and culture, on the one hand, and in close touch with the Anglo world, on the other.[28]

In 1966 Warshauer reported Spanish accounted for two-thirds of the foreign-language broadcasting in the United States, more than would be anticipated on the size of the Latino population.[29] She also found that Spanish-language programming did not follow trends of other foreign-language programs, indicating the uniqueness of the audience and medium merited research as a topic unto itself. She also noted a trend for Spanish-language programs to be found on stations which devote a large portion of their program day to it, rather than only in isolated periods.

Finally, in 1970 Grebler, Moore and Guzmán noted that use of Spanish-language radio was tied to "Mexicanness" of neighborhood in surveys they took in San Antonio and Los Angeles. They also noted that almost all announcers on Spanish-language broadcast stations came from Latin America, in spite of the growth of the Chicano audience. They wrote:

> A sidelight is that almost all announcers on Spanish-language stations—radio and television—are imported from Mexico or other Latin-American countries. The complaint is that the American version of Spanish is either too pocho (i.e., too intermixed with English words or constructions) or too "peasanty" (i.e., agricul-

11

tural terms are used in discussing nonagricultural subjects). Local Mexican Americans are used only in "personality" spots.[30]

Spanish-language radio continued to change in the 1960s. Personality radio was still strong in some regions of the Southwest, especially in communities where Chicanos were used to waking up to the same disc jockey for years. But in the larger cities a more tightly packaged format sound gained strength among Spanish-language broadcasters. Under the format arrangement the music is selected by the station management to convey a consistent musical sound that the audience will find throughout the broadcast day. On these stations the disc jockey has less control over selection of music but is responsible for announcing and playing pre-recorded commercials and other announcements. Thus, the sound of Spanish-language radio is not unlike a number of other music oriented English-language stations; with an emphasis on music and a minimum of talk.

As Spanish-language radio approached the 1970s it was a strong component of the United States broadcast system and accounted for the majority of foreign-language programs in the United States. But it was not without problems. The potential competition of Spanish-language television, which had developed over the 1960s, was one threat. Another was the aging of the listeners who had provided much of the audience base during the 1940s, 1950s and 1960s. Finally, as stations sought more advertising from larger corporations they found they had to use increasingly sophisticated techniques to attract the advertising revenues. The old days when the broker could visit each advertiser to personally sell and collect were gone.

Spanish-language Radio Today

Despite the competition from Spanish-language television and other problems, Spanish-language radio continued to grow through the 1970s. It was growth marked by an increasing attention to format programming on the air and to sophisticated marketing techniques on the business side. As Spanish-language radio stations competed for the attention of national advertising accounts they became more dependent on audience demographics, rating services, census figures, and other marketing devices to make the sale. Some advertising agencies such as Young and Rubicam opened special divisions to deal with the increasing ethnic market. In addition, a string of specialty agencies, such as Spanish Advertising and Marketing Services, Don Passante Associates, Med-Mark, Conill Advertising Associates, Caballero Spanish Media, and others, exerted increasing influence on advertisers desiring to reach the Latino customer. For many advertisers, radio had distinct advantages as an advertising medium to the Latino community. A 1972 article in *Media Decisions* commented:

> Radio continues to have all the elements to make it a very strong communications link between marketers and the U.S. Spanish market. It's ubiquitous. It's oral. It has the capability of establishing strong personal rapport with the local ethnic community.[31]

Some marketers also perceived an advantage of Spanish-language radio over Spanish-language television in reaching bilingual Latinos, the most rapidly growing linguistic segment of the Latino population. Edmundo Bermudez, whose Bermundez Associates consults with major advertising agencies and advertisers hoping to reach Latino consumers, was quoted in a 1977 article:

> Television and radio combined is the best way to reach the Latino audience, in part because of a lack of magazines and newspapers. ... The market is primarily made up of immigrants. At first they watch Spanish TV. As they become comfortable with English, they add U.S. TV. But they don't abandon Spanish radio. Even when we Latinos are comfortable with English, we listen to Spanish radio for the music if not so much for the language."[32]

Spanish-language radio profited by the increased infusion of advertising dollars into Spanish-language media by large corporations eager to capture the Latino customer. The number of stations offering Spanish-language programs increased during the 1970's with the growth of the population and the advertising revenues. According to some sources, the quality of news, public affairs, and consumer reporting also improved on Spanish-language stations during the 1970s.[33]

As the proportion of Latinos grew in major metropolitan areas of the United States, the Spanish-language radio stations improved their relative positions with English-language stations in audience ratings reports, despite problems with accurate sampling techniques.[34] One marketing magazine reported Spanish-language stations were the number one stations in two cities and "jockey for fourth and fifth in others."[35] *Television/Radio Age* described what happened when some advertisers started accounts with San Antonio's KCOR and Miami's WQBA, not knowing they were Spanish because they were top stations in audience ratings:

> They didn't even know they were Spanish. They bought them be-

cause they had the first or second biggest numbers in their markets. They found out what was going on only when the stations called back and said they couldn't run the commercials unless they were translated into Spanish first.[36]

The growing strength of Southwestern Spanish-language radio stations as measured by advertising revenues and audience position, was also indicated by the growing price tag on the Spanish-language stations in a period of active station trading. In 1977 the estate of Paco Sánchez sold Denver's KFSC (now KBNO) for half a million dollars.[37] Top prices were also paid in the mid-1970s for San Francisco's KOFY ($800,000),[38] Salinas' KCTY ($605,437),[39] San Antonio's KCOR and KQXT ($2,400,000),[40] and Los Angeles' KLVE ($2,000,000).[41]

The importance and impact of Spanish-language radio continued to grow through the 1970s because its programming was designed to attract a growing ethnic audience in a medium (radio) that is increasingly oriented to reaching smaller segments of the general population.[42] This growth has been abetted by an increased emphasis on market segmentation by advertisers and marketers.[43] Thus, Spanish-language radio will continue to grow and prosper as long as it is able to attract an audience that advertisers want to reach.

The ability of Spanish-language radio to continue to attract the Latino audience is both supported and questioned by the most recent studies. A 1977 *Sales & Marketing Management* article cautioned:

> Use of a Spanish broadcast medium should be supplemented with "Anglo" stations. Arbitron (a rating service) studies listening time shares show that 45% of all Latinos' radio listening time is spent with Spanish radio stations, meaning that more than half of their time goes for non-Spanish outlets. Spanish teens show even more striking contrasts. They devote 61.3% of their listening time to contemporary-music stations vs. only 13.8% for Spanish stations; in fact, they spend as much time listening to black radio, 11.8%, as to the Spanish version.[44]

But, although Spanish-language radio's hold on the potentially crucial young Latino may be weakening, the medium continues to be strong in other segments of the Latino population, particularly among Chicanos. During the 1970s a number of studies on Chicano media use have documented that Spanish-language radio has been and continues to be an important means of communication throughout the Southwest.[45]

There is also some indication in these studies by scholars that Spanish-language radio may be more heavily preferred by lower income Chicanos, those most dependent on Spanish, and those most culturally linked with Mexico; sectors of the Chicano community which can probably be described as facing the most severe discrimination. For instance, in a 1973 survey of Chicano media use in San Antonio and Austin, Texas, Valenzuela found Chicanos of lower socio-economic status had a significant preference for Spanish-language radio over English-language radio when compared with Chicanos in higher socio-economic groups.[46] Thus, Spanish-language radio continues to be a strong medium of communication for Chicanos, but it is also a medium that appears to be most heavily used by members of the Chicano community who are the weakest economically and politically. Therefore, it would appear that Spanish-language broadcasters have a special responsibility to the needs of their audience for information to assist in improving their lives and communities.

The Purpose of the Book

The following chapters present information on how Spanish-language radio operates based on research conducted by the authors over a five-year period in the 1970s. The study looks at Spanish-language radio from the perspective of members of the audience with the goal of providing greater understanding of the characteristics of Spanish-language radio and how it is operated in the Southwest. It is hoped that by sharing this information with others that a greater understanding of the importance of Spanish-language radio in the Southwest will be developed. The remainder of the book is divided into five chapters: (1) Spanish-language Radio in the United States; (2) Spanish-language Radio in the Southwest; Patterns of Ownership, Employment and Wealth; (3) Comparison of News and Public Affairs on a Spanish and an English-language Station; (4) A Case Study of Spanish-language Station XXX; and (5) Conclusions.

NOTES

[1]For compilations of demographic information on Latinos with special attention to media trends see "Spanish-language Market Study," *Television/Radio Age*, November 7, 1977, pp. S-1–S-24; Joseph Aguayo, "Latinos: Los Que Importan Son Ustedes," *Sales & Marketing Management*, July 11, 1977, pp. 23–29; and "So They All Speak Spanish," *Media Decisions*, May 1977, pp. 68–71, 116.

[2]*Broadcasting Yearbook 1973* (Washington, D.C.: Broadcasting Publications, Inc., 1973), pp. D-51–D-52.

[3]*Broadcasting Yearbook 1978* (Washington, D.C.: Broadcasting Publications, Inc., in 1978), pp. D-85 and D-95–D-96.

[4]*Broadcasting Yearbook 1978*, op. cit., pp. B-143—B-144.

[5]See Glenn Armon, "Minorities Market Ethnic Broadcasters Make an Effective Pitch," *Barrons*, September 3, 1973, pp. 3, 8; and "Usefulness of Spanish Stations Driven Home to Advertisers," *Television/Radio Age*, September 29, 1975, (Reprint) and "Habla Usted Español?," *Newsweek*, June 11, 1973 (Reprint).

[6]"Those Spanish-language 11 Million," *Media Decisions*, March 1972, p. 119.

[7]"Spanish-language Market Study," op. cit., p. S-6.

[8]"Success Stories, Research Help Spanish Station Sales," *Television/Radio Age*, November 7, 1977, pp. S-17, S-19.

[9]See Jorge Reina Schement and Ricardo Flores, "The Origins of Spanish-Language Radio: The Case of San Antonio, Texas," *Journalism History*, Summer 1977, p. 56.

[10]Robert J. Landry, *This Fascinating Radio Business* (Indianapolis-New York: The Bobbs-Merrill Company, 1946), p. 128.

[11]Schement and Flores, op. cit., p. 56.

[12]Rodolfo Hoyos, Sr., interview, Los Angeles, March 26, 1974.

[13]"Spanish Program Firm," *Broadcasting*, June 15, 1939, p. 68.

[14]Rudolf Arnheim and Martha Collins Bayne, "Foreign Language Broadcasts Over Local American Stations," in Paul F. Lazarsfeld and Frank N. Stanton, *Radio Research 1941* (New York: Duell, Sloan and Pearce, 1941), p. 7.

[15]Ibid., pp. 42–45.

[16]Ibid., pp. 56–57.

[17]See U.S. Office of Censorship, *Code of Wartime Practices for American Broadcasters*, Washington, D.C., Editions of June 15, 1942, February 1, 1943, December 1, 1943, and May 15, 1943. Also "Foreign Language Radio to Clean Up," *Variety*, May 20, 1942, p. 26; Carl J. Friedrich, "Foreign Language Radio and the War," *Common Ground*, Autumn 1942, pp. 65–72; Ben Bodec, "Foreign Stations 'Confess,'" *Variety*, May 20, 1942, p. 31–32; and Edward Jenks, "What Are They Saying," *New York Times*, June 28, 1942, Sect. VII, p. 10.

[18]See "Licensee Responsibility to Exercise Adequate Control Over Foreign Language Programs," *Federal Communications Commission Reports*, 39 F.C.C. 2d, pp. 1037–1042 and "Strict Checks Not Needed for Non-English Programs," *Broadcasting*, March 19, 1973, p. 126. Controls required of stations carrying foreign-language broadcasts are not required of those carrying only English-language programs, although they are a relaxation of the controls imposed by the FCC in "Broadcasters Cautioned to Exercise Adequate Control Over Foreign Language Programs," FCC 67–368, Public Notice-B, March 30, 1967.

[19]Landry, op. cit., pp. 253–254.

[20]Schement and Flores, op. cit., p. 57.

[21]James Coyle, interview, Salinas, California, August 11, 1974.

[22]"Hispanos Have Small Voice in Radio Broadcasting," *Denver Post*, December 23, 1972 (Reprint).

[23]Schement and Flores, op. cit.

[24]Jane MacNab Christian and Chester C. Christian, Jr., "Spanish Language and Culture in the Southwest" in Joshua A. Fishman, *Language Loyalty in the United States* (The Hague: Mouton & Co., 1966), p. 297.

[25]*Sponsor* magazine carried an annual report on Spanish-language broadcasting each October for much of the 1960s. The report included both articles and listings of stations. For one example of the annual report see *Sponsor*, October 19, 1965.

See also "Spanish Market: Undersold, Undervalued," Special Report, *Broadcasting*, September 19, 1966, pp. 67–90.

26Robert Somerville Graham, "Spanish-language Radio in Northern Colorado," *American Speech*, October 1962, p. 211.

27Christian and Christian, op. cit., p. 296.

28Ibid., p. 297.

29Mary Ellen Warshauer, "Foreign Language Broadcasting" in Joshua A. Fishman, op. cit., p. 86.

30Leo Grebler, Joan Moore and Ralph Guzmán, *The Mexican American People* (New York: The Free Press, 1970), pp. 431–432.

31"Those Spanish Language 11 Million," *Media Decisions*, March 1972, p. 122.

32"So They All Speak Spanish, op. cit., p. 69.

33"Spanish-language Market Study, op. cit, p. S-20.

34See "Usefulness of Spanish Stations Driven Home to Advertisers," *Television/Radio Age*, September 29, 1975, (Reprint) and "Station Rankings to Shift in Ethnic-rating Storm?" *Television/Radio Age*, February 19, 1973, pp. 23–25, 68–71.

35Dan Rustin, "The Spanish Market: Its Size, Income and Loyalties Make It a Rich Marketing Mine," *Television/Radio Age*, October 2, 1972, (Reprint).

36"Spanish-language Market Study," op. cit., p. S-18.

37"Changing Hands," *Broadcasting*, September 26, 1977, p. 33.

38"Changing Hands," *Broadcasting*, April 5, 1976, p. 49.

39"Changing Hands," *Broadcasting*, December 8, 1975, p. 40.

40"Changing Hands," *Broadcasting*, July 14, 1975, p. 49.

41"Changing Hands," *Broadcasting*, October 6, 1975, p. 36.

42Kenneth A. Longman, *Advertising* (New York: Harcourt Brace, Javanovich, Inc. 1972), p. 218 and Sydney W. Head, *Broadcasting in America* (Boston: Houghton Mifflin Company, 1972), pp. 217–223.

43Philip Kotler, *Marketing Management* (Englewood Cliffs: Prentice-Hall, Inc., 1972), pp. 165–166.

44"Latino Media: Available in Any Mood from Conservative to Salsa," *Sales & Marketing Management*, July 11, 1977, p. 25. See also *How Blacks and Spanish Listen to Radio Report 2*, Arbitron Radio, January 1976.

45See Judith M. Rickard, *Media Habits of Mexican-Americans in Eastside San José*, Institute for Business and Economic Research, School of Business, San José State University, 1976; Nicholas Valenzuela, and Herbert S. Dordick, *A Study of Mexican-American Information Sources and Media Usage in Boyle Heights (East Los Angeles)*, Center for Communication Policy Research, University of Southern California, December 1974; Miriam Jean Seger Bundy, "A Comparison of English and Spanish Mass Media Preferences of Mexican Americans in East Los Angeles," Masters Thesis, California State University, Fullerton, 1973; and Nicholas Valenzuela, *Media Habits and Attitudes of Mexican Americans*, Center for Communication Research, University of Texas at Austin, June 1973.

46Valenzuela, op. cit., p. 171.

CHAPTER II

Spanish-language Radio in the United States

The size and nature of Spanish-language radio in the United States and the Southwest is described in this chapter. The information documents the continued growth of Spanish-language radio throughout the United States, its distribution by Latino population centers, and characteristics of ownership, programming, employment, and economics that are important to understanding the direction in which Spanish-language radio continues to grow. The chapter reports the results of a national census of all Spanish-language radio stations in the United States based on information available in *Broadcasting Yearbook* and the Standard Rate and Data Service's *Spot Radio*.

This chapter presents the characteristics of Spanish-language radio nationally, in a single source, for the first time. This information is significant because it gives the reader an understanding of the overall dimensions of a communications medium that is becoming increasingly important for Latinos and the broadcasting industry. The data describe how many stations there are, where they are located in relation to Latino populations, technical characteristics, how many hours of Spanish they program, how they are connected, and who owns, manages, and works for Spanish-language radio. Thus, this chapter paints the broad picture of Spanish-language radio at the national level that helps put the smaller units discussed in subsequent chapters into perspective.

Selection of Stations

Both the *Broadcasting Yearbook* and *Spot Radio* were used to develop the list of 485 Spanish-language radio stations used in this study.*
The *Yearbook*, an annually updated guide to broadcasting in the United

---

* The methodology is described in the Appendix.

States, lists Spanish radio programming in both its descriptions of the programming on each radio station in the United States and its listing of programming formats and the different stations broadcasting them. *Spot Radio* has a listing of Spanish-language radio stations and was used as a secondary reference. Stations included in the census are those which were described as broadcasting all or part of their programming in Spanish in either publication.

The two sources revealed 485 radio stations broadcasting all or part of their programs in Spanish in the United States. However, it should be noted at the outset that the 485 stations do not represent all of the radio stations broadcasting in Spanish to audiences in the United States. The same sources indicated at least 35 Mexican Spanish-language stations broadcast to audiences that include Chicanos in the Southwestern United States. The *Yearbook* lists 35 Mexican Spanish-language stations near or along the border that have sales representatives specializing in reaching U.S. Spanish-language audiences. *Spot Radio* includes a number of Mexican Spanish-language border stations in its listings of stations serving U.S. communities along the border. These Mexican-licensed Spanish-language radio stations broadcast to Chicano audiences in San Diego, Calexico, Yuma, Nogales, El Paso, Brownsville, McAllen, Del Rio, Laredo, Eagle Pass and their surrounding areas.

Since Mexican and United States radio stations are covered by different national laws, no single source of information could provide comparable information on both sets of stations. Therefore, it was not possible to analyze and compare information on the Mexican stations in this survey. Because of this, the Mexican licensed Spanish-language radio stations remain a component of Spanish-language broadcasting that remains to be more fully researched.

The analysis of programming on the 485 stations (to be discussed more fully in a later section) revealed that most of the stations broadcasting programs in Spanish did so only a few hours a week. Of the 485 radio stations (about 6% of the stations listed in the *Yearbook*), only 55 (11%) broadcast more than half of their programming in Spanish (see Table 1). The remaining stations either broadcast Spanish for less than half of their time (88%) or provided insufficient information for classification (1%). For purposes of this study those stations broadcasting half or more of their hours in Spanish are called Primary Spanish Language Radio (PSLR). Those broadcasting less than half their hours in Spanish are called Secondary Spanish Language Radio (SSLR).

Physical Characteristics

An analysis of Spanish-language radio stations by location identified

TABLE 1: Frequency Distribution of Primary and Secondary
Spanish Radio Stations

Classification	Number	Percent
Primary Spanish (Fifty percent or more of hours in Spanish)	55	11
Secondary Spanish (Less than fifty percent of hours in Spanish)	425	88
Unknown (Percent of Spanish hours not known)	5	1
Total	485	100

Source: *Broadcasting Yearbook.*

stations in 38 states and the District of Columbia (see Table 2A). The only states with no radio stations programming any time in Spanish were Alaska, Delaware, Hawaii, Kentucky, Maine, Maryland, Mississippi, New Hampshire. Rhode Island, South Carolina, Vermont and West Virginia. It was also found that the distribution of Spanish-language radio stations roughly follows the geographic dispersion of Latinos in the United States.

The largest number of stations were found in the states with the highest concentrations of Latinos (see Table 2B). This is particularly true of PSLR stations, which are more highly concentrated in states with high Latino population figures than SSLR stations. For instance, Texas and California, the two states with the largest Latino populations, account for 64% of all PSLR stations but only 36% of all Spanish-language stations.

The correlation between Latino residential patterns and Spanish-language radio stations is further demonstrated by examining the distribution of these stations in cities located in the top 50 Latino Standard Metropolitan Statistical Areas (SMSAs) in the U.S. Of the 485 stations, 153 (32%) were located in one of the top 50 Latino SMSAs and 45 of these stations were PSLR (see Table 3A). These 45 stations comprise about 80% of all PSLR stations in the nation. As in the state tabulation, the distribution of SSLR stations is more widely dispersed among the Latino SMSAs, indicating more radio stations commit fewer hours to Spanish-language programming where fewer Latinos live. The statistical significance of the different distribution patterns of PSLR and SSLR stations was compared by the Chi Square test for independence of cells and found to be significant to the .001 level (see Table 3B).

In summary, 485 stations were identified as broadcasting Spanish in the United States. Of these only 11% programmed Spanish more than

21

Frequency Distribution of Spanish-language Radio Stations by State

State	Percent	Number	State	Percent	Number
Alabama	00	1	Missouri	00	1
Alaska	----	----	Montana	----	1
Arizona	3	15	Nebraska	1	4
Arkansas	1	3	Nevada	1	3
California	17	82	New Hampshire	----	----
Colorado	5	26	New Jersey	2	11
Connecticut	4	17	New Mexico	5	24
Delaware	----	----	New York	4	18
D.C.	00	2	North Carolina	00	1
Florida	3	12	North Dakota	00	1
Georgia	1	4	Ohio	3	12
Hawaii	----	----	Oklahoma	00	2
Idaho	2	11	Oregon	1	5
Illinois	5	23	Pennsylvania	2	9
Indiana	2	8	Rhode Island	----	----
Iowa	1	4	South Carolina	----	----
Kansas	2	11	South Dakota	00	1
Kentucky	----	----	Tennessee	00	2
Louisiana	00	1	Texas	19	93
Maine	----	----	Utah	2	9
Maryland	----	----	Vermont	----	----
Massachusetts	3	13	Virginia	00	1
Michigan	5	23	Washington	3	12
Minnesota	00	2	West Virginia	----	----
Mississippi	----	----	Wisconsin	2	10
			Wyoming	1	10
			Total	100	485

Source: *Broadcasting Yearbook.*

TABLE 2B: Frequency Distribution of Spanish-language Radio Stations
by State as Ranked by Percentage of Latino Population

State	Percent of Latino Population	Number of Primary Stations	Number of Secondary Stations	Number of Unknown Stations	Total Stations	Percent of Stations
California	26	18	64	0	82	17
Texas	20	17	76	0	93	19
New York	15	2	16	0	18	4
Florida	4	3	9	0	12	3
Illinois	4	2	19	2	23	5
New Mexico	3	5	18	1	24	5
New Jersey	3	0	11	0	11	2
Arizona	3	4	11	0	15	3
Colorado	2	2	24	0	26	5

State	Percent of Latino Population	Number of Primary Stations	Number of Secondary Stations	Number of Unknown Stations	Total Stations	Percent of Stations
Michigan	2	0	22	1	23	5
Ohio	1	0	11	1	12	3
Indiana	1	0	8	0	8	2
Pennsylvania	1	0	9	0	9	2
Louisiana	1	0	1	0	1	----
Massachusetts	1	0	13	0	13	3
Connecticut	1	1	16	0	17	4
Wisconsin	1	0	10	0	10	2
Missouri	1	0	1	0	1	----
Washington	1	0	12	0	12	3
Kansas	1	0	11	0	11	2
Oklahoma	1	0	2	0	2	----
Tennessee	1	0	2	0	2	----
Maryland	1	0	0	0	0	0
Georgia	----	0	4	0	4	1
Kentucky	----	0	0	0	0	0
North Carolina	----	0	1	0	0	----
Virginia	----	0	1	0	1	----
Alabama	----	0	1	0	1	----
Minnesota	----	0	2	0	2	----
Utah	----	0	9	0	9	2
Hawaii	----	0	0	0	0	0
Arkansas	----	0	3	0	3	1
Oregon	----	0	5	0	5	1
Iowa	----	4	0	0	4	1
Nebraska	----	4	0	0	4	1
Nevada	----	0	3	0	3	1
Idaho	----	0	11	0	11	2
Mississippi	----	0	0	0	0	0
D. C.	----	1	1	0	2	----
South Carolina	----	0	0	0	0	0
Wyoming	----	0	7	0	7	1
West Virginia	----	0	0	0	0	0
Delaware	----	0	0	0	0	0
Rhode Island	----	0	0	0	0	0
Montana	----	0	1	0	1	----
Alaska	----	0	0	0	0	0
South Dakota	----	0	1	0	1	----
North Dakota	----	0	1	0	1	----
Maine	----	0	0	0	0	0
New Hampshire	----	0	0	0	0	0
Vermont	----	0	0	0	0	0
Total	95	55	425	5	485	100

Source: *1970 Census and Broadcasting Yearbook.*

TABLE 3A. Frequency Distribution of Spanish-language Radio Stations
in the Top 50 Latino Standard Metropolitan Statistical
Areas (SMSA)

SMSA	Number of Primary Stations	Number of Secondary Stations	Number of Unknown Stations	Total Stations	Percent of Stations
New York	2	2	0	4	1
Los Angeles/Long Beach	2	4	0	6	1
San Antonio	3	1	0	4	1
San Francisco/Oakland	2	3	0	5	1
Chicago	2	13	2	17	4
Miami	3	3	0	6	1
Houston	1	5	0	6	1
El Paso	1	1	0	2	----
San Bernardino/Riverside	1	1	0	2	----
San Jose	2	0	0	2	----
San Diego	0	3	0	3	1
Anaheim/Santa Ana/ Garden Grove	0	0	0	0	0
Dallas/Fort Worth	1	2	0	3	1
McAllen/Pharr/Edinburg	1	1	0	2	----
Phoenix	1	2	0	3	1
Denver/Boulder	1	4	0	5	1
Albuquerque	3	0	0	3	1
Corpus Christi	3	1	0	4	1
Brownsville/Harlingen/ San Benito	1	0	0	1	----
Fresno	2	1	0	3	1
Newark	0	5	0	5	1
Jersey City	0	0	0	0	0
Philadelphia	0	3	0	3	1
Tucson	3	2	0	5	1
Sacramento	1	4	0	5	1
Nassau/Suffolk	0	1	0	1	----
Oxnard/Simi Valley/ Ventura	1	0	0	1	----
D. C.	1	1	0	2	----
Laredo	0	1	0	1	----
Tampa/St. Petersberg	0	1	0	1	----
Detroit	0	3	1	4	1
Bakersfield	2	1	0	3	1
Austin	0	2	0	2	----
Salinas/Seaside/Monterey	1	2	0	3	1
Stockton	2	2	0	4	1
Visalia	0	1	0	1	----
Santa Barbara/Santa Maria/Lompoc	0	8	0	8	2

24

SMSA	Number of Primary Stations	Number of Secondary Stations	Number of Unknown Stations	Total Stations	Percent of Stations
			TABLE 3A. (Continued)		
New Orleans	0	1	0	1	----
Pueblo	1	1	0	2	----
Boston	0	5	0	5	1
Gary/Hammond/East Chicago	0	3	0	3	1
Salt Lake City	0	2	0	2	----
Paterson/Clifton/Passaic	0	0	0	0	0
Lubbock	1	2	0	3	1
Kansas City	0	1	0	1	----
Modesto	0	2	0	2	----
Vallejo/Fairfield/Napa	0	1	0	1	----
Seattle/Everett	0	1	0	1	----
Milwaukee	0	1	0	1	----
St. Louis	0	1	0	1	----
Total Spanish SMSA	45	105	3	153	32
Total Not In Spanish SMSA	10	32	2	332	68
Total	55	425	5	485	100

Source: *Broadcasting Yearbook* and *Spot Radio*.

TABLE 3B: Crosstabulation of Spanish by Latino SMSA

	Primary Spanish (N=55)	Secondary Spanish (N=425)
Major Latino SMSA	82%	25%
Non-Major Latino SMA	18	75

Source: *Broadcasting Yearbook*.   S = .001

half of their broadcast time. It was also shown that Spanish programming was found in 38 states, but was most highly concentrated in states and metropolitan areas with the highest Latino populations. This was particularly true of the PSLR stations.

While establishing a relationship between the distribution of Spanish-language radio stations and the distribution of Latinos in the United States might appear to be an unnecessary task, it is actually very important. This is because it establishes that Spanish-language radio is primarily designed to address the Latino community in this country and not for other purposes, such as language instruction or cultural enhancement.

Technical Characteristics

Technical characteristics of Spanish-language radio broadcasting are those engineering aspects of a station's operation that are regulated by the Federal Communications Commission (FCC). These include spectrum, type of station, hours of broadcast, and service class. These characteristics were examined for two reasons: (1) to describe the technical characteristics of Spanish-language radio and (2) to compare differences between PSLR and SSLR stations. The comparison between PSLR and SSLR stations was made to determine if there are significances in the level of technical service offered by the two types of stations. Since SSLR stations are essentially English-language stations programming only a few hours in Spanish, it was felt they would provide a basis for comparing English-language and Spanish-language stations. Thus, the analysis would show whether allocation of technical resources was equal between the two kinds of stations or if there was an unequal distribution to the advantage of one or the other. Differences were compared by the Chi Square test for independence of cells and only differences reported significant to the .10 level are reported.

AM or FM. The stations were first coded to determine how many were on the AM or FM spectrum. It was found that of the 485 stations 363 (75%) were AM, 113 (23%) were FM, and nine (2%) broadcast on both frequencies (see Table 4). The nine stations classified as both AM and FM were removed from the analysis of technical characteristics of AM and FM stations.

Commercial or Non-Commercial. The stations were also coded to determine whether they were licensed as commercial or non-commer-

TABLE 4: Frequency Distribution of Spanish-language Radio Stations by AM and FM

Category	Number	Percent
AM	363	75
FM	113	23
Both	9	2
Totals	485	100

Source: *Broadcasting Yearbook.*

cial radio stations (see Table 5A). Of the 485 stations in the survey, 416 (86%) are commercial stations and 69 (14%) non-commercial. The comparison of PSLR and SSLR stations showed that all of the primary Spanish stations were commercial while of the secondary Spanish stations 84% were commercial and 16% non-commercial (see Table 5B). FM stations are additionally designated between educational and commercial frequencies. Educational frequencies are limited to the bottom end of the FM spectrum (88 to 92 megacycles) and about half of them are limited to 10 watts of power. A comparison of FM PSLR and SSLR stations revealed significant differences, with all of the PSLR stations broadcasting commercially and most of the SSLR stations educationally (see Table 5C).

Full Time and Part Time. The Federal Communications Commission (FCC) limits AM radio stations by authorizing some to broadcast full time (24 hours a day) and others part time (daytime only or shortened broadcast days). Analysis of the AM stations revealed 193 (53%) of them were authorized for full time service, about the same as the national average[1] (see Table 6A). However, when PSLR and SSLR stations were compared significant differences were found (see Table 6B). The analysis revealed 64% of the PSLR stations were unable to broadcast at night or had other restricted hours, while 36% of the SSLR stations were so restricted.

Service Class. The FCC authorizes radio stations to operate in certain service classes, which generally indicate the power, antenna, operating hours, and other restrictions stations must follow. Since AM and FM stations are classified differently by service class they were analyzed separately.

AM stations are classified as Class I, which means they have full-time high power as a clear channel or dominant station; as Class II or Class III, which means that they have lower power, are subordinate stations on the frequency, may have directional antennas, and reduced or no

TABLE 5A: Frequency Distribution of Spanish-language Stations by Commercial or Non-Commercial

Category	Number	Percent
Commercial	416	86
Non-Commercial	69	14
Totals	485	100

Source: *Broadcasting Yearbook.*

TABLE 5B: Crosstabulation of Spanish by Commercial/Non-Commercial

Category	Primary Spanish (N=55)	Secondary Spanish (N=425)
Commercial	100%	84%
Non-Commercial	0	16

Source: *Broadcasting Yearbook.*   S=.001

TABLE 5C: Crosstabulation of Spanish by FM Frequency Type

Frequency Type	Primary Spanish (N=11)	Secondary Spanish (N=98)
88–92: Limited to Educational Uses	0%	58%
92–106: Not Limited to Educational Uses	100	42

Source: *Broadcasting Yearbook.*   S=.001

TABLE 6A: Frequency Distribution of AM Spanish-language Stations by Fulltime or Parttime Service

Category	Number	Percent
Fulltime	193	53
Parttime	169	47
Totals	362	100

Source: *Broadcasting Yearbook.*

TABLE 6B: Crosstabulation of Spanish by AM Fulltime or Parttime

Category	Primary Spanish (N=44)	Secondary Spanish (N=318)
Fulltime	36%	56%
Parttime	64	44

Source: *Broadcasting Yearbook.*   S=.05

night power; or as Class IV, which means they are lower power stations authorized for full-time broadcasting to a local community. Class I stations have highest power and few restrictions. Class II and III stations have lower power and/or more restrictions. Class IV stations have lowest power, but few other restrictions.

A tabulation of AM stations by service class revealed that 262 (72%) of the 362 AM stations broadcasting Spanish are classified as Class II or III stations (see Table 7A). A crosstabulation of AM class by Spanish showed that 89% of the AM PSLR stations are in Classes II and III, while only 69% of the SSLR stations are in the same categories (see Table 7B). Neither has a strong percentage in the Class I stations, but 30% of the secondary stations are authorized for full-time local service (Class IV) as opposed to only 11% of the primary stations. Chi Square analysis of the crosstabulation revealed the differences significant to the .10 level.

FM radio stations are also restricted by service class. Class A FM radio stations are licensed to serve small communities and are limited to 3,000 watts of broadcast power. Class B and C FM stations are licensed to serve larger areas and may be granted up to 100,000 watts of broadcast power. FM educational stations are licensed for non-commercial use and were originally authorized for under 10 watts of power. However, they may now apply for greater power if they so desire.

TABLE 7A: Frequency Distribution of AM Spanish-language Stations by Service Class

Class	Number	Percent
Class I	1	----
Class II	99	27
Class III	163	45
Class IV	97	27
Totals	360*	99*

Source: *Broadcasting Yearbook.*
*Two stations have missing information.

TABLE 7B: *Crosstabulation of Spanish by AM Service Class*

Class	Primary Spanish (N=44)	Secondary Spanish (N=316)
Class I	0%	----%
Class II	39	26
Class III	50	45
Class IV	11	29
Totals	100%	100%

Source: *Broadcasting Yearbook.*   S=.10

An analysis of the 109 FM stations revealed a majority of these stations broadcasting Spanish are non-commercial (see Table 7C). When PSLR and SSLR stations were compared it was found that, while representation for both types was about equal in Class A FM stations, there is an overrepresentation of PSLR stations in Classes A and B and underrepresentation on non-commercial when compared with SSLR stations (see Table 7D). This indicates a strong representation of PSLR stations in FM classes with the widest power, but none in the non-commercial category.

Summary of Technical Characteristics. The analysis of technical characteristics reveals Spanish-language radio to be concentrated primarily on the AM band (75% of all Spanish-language stations) and on commercial stations (86%). Primary Spanish stations were found only in the commercial category, indicating there were no primary Spanish-language non-commercial or educational stations at the time of the survey. The survey also revealed that when primary and secondary Spanish-language stations were compared the primary stations were generally found in the less desirable categories in number of broadcast hours and broadcast service class.

TABLE 7C: Frequency Distribution of FM Spanish-language Stations by Service Class

Service Class	Number	Percent
Class A	18	17
Class B or C	33	30
Non-Commercial	58	53
Totals	109	100

Source: *Broadcasting Yearbook.*

TABLE 7D: Crosstabulation of Spanish by FM Service Class

Service Class	Primary Spanish (N=11)	Secondary Spanish (N=98)
Class A	18%	16%
Class B or C	82	25
FM Non Commercial	0	59
Totals	100%	100%

Source: *Broadcasting Yearbook.*   S=.001

Network Characteristics

Network characteristics as reported in *Broadcasting Yearbook* and *Spot Radio* were also analyzed to determine if stations were affiliated with a national or regional radio network (which would provide programming and/or advertising), whether the station lists a regional or national sales representative (indicating it seeks advertising outside its local market), and whether or not the station is affiliated with a network specializing in Spanish-language stations.

Network. The analysis revealed that 259 (51%) of the stations programming Spanish are affiliated with a national and/or regional network (see Table 8A). When PSLR and SSLR stations were compared by affiliation it was found that primary Spanish stations were significantly underrepresented in terms of network affiliation, while secondary Spanish stations were closer to the overall breakdown (see Table 8B).

National and Regional Representatives. National and regional representatives are sales agencies that represent local radio and television

TABLE 8A: Frequency Distribution of Spanish-language Radio Stations by Network Affiliation

Network Affiliation	Number	Percent
One National Network	155	32
Two National Network	9	2
One National, One Regional	35	7
Two National, One Regional	5	1
Three National, One Regional	1	----
One National, Two Regional	2	----
One Regional Network	42	9
Sub Total	249	51
No Network Listed	236	49
Total	485	100

Source: *Broadcasting Yearbook.*

TABLE 8B: Crosstabulation of Spanish by Network

Network	Primary Spanish (N=55)	Secondary Spanish (N=425)
Network Affiliated	16%	44%
Not Network Affiliated	84	56

Source: *Broadcasting Yearbook.* S=.001

31

stations in securing advertising from outside their market. Most representatives represent a string of stations and work on a commission based on the amount of advertising secured for the stations. Such representation is important to local stations seeking advertising from outside their service area. The representatives also simplify billing and placement procedures for national advertisers seeking to reach the segmented markets represented by radio audiences.

The analysis revealed that 296 stations (61%) are affiliated with national or regional representatives (see Table 9A). When PSLR and SSLR stations were compared by affiliation with a representative it was found that primary Spanish stations were overrepresented in the affiliated category, while secondary Spanish stations were less heavily represented and were closer to the overall breakdown (see Table 9B).

Spanish Network/Representative. Some Spanish-language radio stations are affiliated with sales representatives specializing in securing advertising for Spanish-language radio. These strings of stations are listed as "networks" in the *Broadcasting Yearbook*, although they actually provide no programming to the stations. The *Yearbook* lists nine such networks and the stations represented by each. Some stations are listed with more than one network and most networks include stations in Mexico.

Analysis revealed that 51% of the PSLR and 3% of the SSLR were affiliated with Spanish networks, that the Amigo Spanish Group, a network established by the Savalli/Gates agency, had the highest number of PSLR stations (9) and that the National Spanish Language Network, a network established by National Time Sales, had the highest number of SSLR stations (7) and total stations (14) (see Table

TABLE 9A: Frequency Distribution of Spanish-language Radio Stations by Sales Representatives

Number of Representatives	Number	Percent
One Representative	209	43
Two Representatives	66	14
Three Representatives	16	3
Four Representatives	4	1
Five Representatives	1	----
No representative	189	39
Total	485	100

Source: *Broadcasting Yearbook.*

TABLE 9B: Crosstabulation of Spanish by Sales Representatives

Representative	Primary Spanish (N=55)	Secondary Spanish (N=325)
Has Representative	76%	60%
No Representative	24	40

Source: *Broadcasting Yearbook.*   S = .05

10A). When PSLR and SSLR stations were compared by whether or not they were affiliated with a Spanish network, the analysis revealed that the secondary Spanish stations were significantly underrepresented when compared with the primary stations (see Table 10B).

Summary of Network Characteristics. Network characteristics were explored to determine the extent to which radio stations programming

TABLE 10A: Frequency Distribution of Spanish-language Radio Stations by Spanish Network/Representative

Network Representative	Number of Primary Spanish	Number of Secondary Spanish
AAA California Spanish Network	3	0
AAA Español Network	5	1
All Spanish Network	2	1
Amigo Spanish Group	9	1
Latin Network	6	2
National Spanish Language Network	7	7
Texas Spanish Language Network	3	2
Tichenor Radio Group	3	0
No Spanish Network Representative	27	413
Total	65*	427

Source: *Broadcasting Yearbook.*
*(Several stations are represented by more than one Spanish Network/Representative.

TABLE 10B: Crosstabulation of Spanish by Spanish Network/Representative

Category	Primary Spanish (N=55)	Secondary Spanish (N=425)
Have Spanish Network/Representative	51%	3%
Don't Have Spanish Network/Representative	49	97

Source: *Broadcasting Yearbook.*   S=.001

Spanish were linked to programming and advertising networks and to each other. The data revealed that network affiliations was light among PSLR stations, but the affiliation with national advertising representatives and Spanish-language representatives were significantly higher for the PSLR stations. Thus, the analysis indicates that the links are primarily along advertising, rather than programming, lines and are primarily for the purpose of securing national advertising for the stations so affiliated.

Programming Characteristics

Program characteristics as reported in *Broadcasting Yearbook* were analyzed to determine the amount and type of programs offered by stations offering Spanish-language programs. This information was considered important since foreign-language programming is often characterized as being found on stations with block programming or segmented formats offering diverse types of programming to different audiences. Thus, the analysis of programming was performed to determine to what extent this is true of stations offering programs in Spanish.

Format. The stations were analyzed according to the format or combination of formats they listed in the *Yearbook*. Format listings vary from station to station. Most stations list only one format. But some list more than one and others none. Stations were coded according to the format or combination of formats they listed in the *Yearbook*. The listings were then recorded to conform with the Radio Advertising Bureau's (RAB) 11 radio program categories (Contemporary, Top 40, Middle of the Road, Standard, Good Music, Classical/Semi-classical, Talk, News, Spanish, Black and Religious)[2] and four other program categories showing a large number of stations in the survey (Variety/Diversified, Educational, Progressive, and Spanish plus other programming) (see Table 11). In this portion of the research PSLR stations were found listing their formats as Spanish, Ethnic, and Spanish with other formats. The analysis revealed that Spanish was heard most often on stations with a Middle of the Road format (25%), followed by Country & Western (18%) and Contemporary (14%).

Number of Hours in Spanish. The number of hours per week that station broadcast in Spanish was analyzed to determine the amount of time that stations listing Spanish devote to Spanish-language programs. Stations were coded by the number of weekly Spanish hours listed in the *Yearbook* or, if insufficient information was provided, in *Spot Radio*. Except for full-time Spanish stations, those with an unknown number of hours were coded unknown.

The analysis revealed that of the 485 stations programming Spanish, 331 (70%) provide only nine hours a week or less of Spanish-language broadcasts (see Table 12A). At the other end of the hourly spectrum 49 stations (9%) offered more than 80 hours a week or are full-time

TABLE 11: Frequency Distribution of Spanish-language
Radio Stations by Format

Format	Number	Percent*
Middle of the Road (MOR)	122	25
Country and Western	89	18
Contemporary	69	14
Variety/Diversified	46	9
Spanish Alone	44	9
Top 40/Rock	26	5
Educational	24	5
Classical/Semiclassical	15	3
Progressive	14	3
Religious	12	2
Talk	11	2
Black/Soul/Rhythm & Blues	11	2
Spanish plus other programming	11	2
News/Public Affairs/Information	10	2
Good Music/Easy Listening	7	1
Standards	2	----
Other Formats	24	5
No Format	62	13

Source: *Broadcasting Yearbook.*
*Percent totals more than 100% because some stations list more than one format.

TABLE 12A: Frequency Distribution of Spanish-language Radio Stations by
Hours of Spanish-language Programming Per Week

Hours Per Week	Number	Percent
Nine hours or less	331	70
Ten to 19 hours	53	11
20 to 29 hours	21	4
30 to 39 hours	11	2
40 to 79 hour	9	2
80 to 139 hours	7	1
140 to 169 hours	6	1
Fulltime Spanish	36	7
Unknown	11	2
Total	485	100

Source: *Broadcasting Yearbook.*

Spanish. Thus, the vast majority of stations offer Spanish only a very few hours a week.

Primary or Secondary Spanish. The 485 radio stations were classified as Primary Spanish Language Radio (PSLR) or Secondary Spanish Language Radio (SSLR) stations based on the percentage of their broadcast time devoted to Spanish programs. PSLR stations program 50% or more of their time in Spanish and numbered 55 (11%) of the stations (see Table 12B). SSLR stations accounted for 425 (88%) of the stations. Five stations (1%) provided insufficient programming information and were so coded. Thus, the analysis reveals that nearly 90% of the stations offering Spanish programs do so only as a secondary format to their other programming. The breakdown between PSLR and SSLR stations was used as the basic variable for crosstabulation across other variables in the national survey of Spanish-language radio stations.

Other Programming. The 485 stations were also analyzed to determine the number of other secondary programs they offered. This analysis was performed because foreign language programs are commonly identified as being heard on stations which block program specialized segments to different audiences. The stations were coded by the number of other specialized programs in addition to Spanish they listed in the *Yearbook.* The analysis revealed that 158 stations (33%) offer Spanish as their only specialized programming and that an additional 126 (26%) offered only Spanish and one other special program (see Table 13). Only 12 stations (3%) offered Spanish in combination with six or more other special programs. Thus, the analysis showed that Spanish is heard primarily on stations that do not block program specialized formats.

Summary of Programming Characteristics. The information on programming revealed that Spanish is heard on radio stations offering a

TABLE 12B: Frequency Distribution of Spanish-language Radio
Stations by Primary or Secondary Spanish

Category	Number	Percent
Primary Spanish	55	11
Secondary Spanish	425	88
Unknown	5	1
Total	485	100

Source: *Broadcasting Yearbook.*

TABLE 13: Frequency Distribution of Spanish-language Radio Stations
by Number of Other Programs

Number of Other Programs	Number	Percent
Spanish Only Other Program	159	33
Spanish Plus One Other Program	128	26
Spanish Plus Two Others	52	11
Spanish Plus Three Others	24	5
Spanish Plus Four Others	13	3
Spanish Plus Five Others	7	1
Spanish Plus Six or More (24 highest)	12	3
Fulltime Spanish	42	9
Unknown	48	10
Total	485	101

Source: *Broadcasting Yearbook.*

number of different primary formats and is most often the only specialized program heard on those stations. It was also shown that 70%
of the stations offer Spanish nine hours a week or less and that only 11%
of the stations offered Spanish as their primary format. Thus, the programming of Spanish can be characterized as being heard only a few
hours a week on stations primarily concerned with programming to
another audience.

Employment Characteristics

Employment information was gathered to determine to management
patterns of stations programming Spanish as they relate to employment of Latinos. Data were gathered from the *Yearbook* on Spanish-
surname personnel in administrative positions on PSLR stations. The
Yearbook lists administrative personnel for positions submitted by the
stations. The number of positions listed varies from station to station,
but usually includes the owner/president and the various administrative or department heads. Only PSLR stations were analyzed because
it was considered unlikely that stations programming only a few hours
of Spanish a week would have significant numbers of Spanish-surnamed
owners or top administrators.

The employees listed by the PSLR stations were coded for presence
of a Spanish or Non-Spanish surname. Surname was selected as the
coding unit because it is the most readily available and identifiable
means of indicating Latinos, although it is not totally reliable. Thus,
these data should be used as an indicator of the participation of Latinos

TABLE 14: Frequency Distribution of Management on Primary Spanish Radio Stations

Category	Number of Stations Reporting	Number of Stations Reporting Spanish-Surnames	Number of Stations Not Reporting Spanish-Surnames	Percent of Stations Reporting Spanish-Surnames
Owner/President	46	10	36	21
Top Management	36	9	24	25
Sales	23	7	17	30
Engineering	23	0	35	0
Programming	36	27	11	75
News	20	14	6	70
Promotion	6	5	1	83

Source: *Broadcasting Yearbook.*   N=55 Primary Spanish Radio Stations

in the management of Spanish-language radio stations. The results of the analysis for the seven job categories usually listed are discussed below and shown on the summary table (see Table 14).

Owner/President. The Owner/President is usually the licensee of the station or the head of the corporation holding the license and indicates the person who heads the station or, in the cases of group ownership, the group owning the station. Forty-six of the 55 PSLR stations listed information in this category. Of these, 10 reported Spanish surname owners or presidents and 36 reported non-Spanish surnames. Thus, only 21% of the PSLR stations reporting were headed by Spanish surnamed individuals.

Top Management. Top management indicates the person responsible for the daily operation of the station. In group owned stations this person is usually titled the vice president and general manager. In locally owned stations he or she is usually called the general manager or station manager. Thirty-six of the 55 PSLR stations listed information in this category. Of these, nine listed Spanish surnames and 24 listed non-Spanish surnames. Thus, only 25% of the PSLR stations reporting had Spanish surnamed top management.

Sales. Sales managers are the individuals responsible for selling advertising time on the stations Most stations list their sales manager, advertising manager or commercial manager in this category. Thirty-three of the 55 PSLR stations listed information in this category. Seven listed Spanish surnames and 17 listed non-Spanish surnames (one listed both). Thus, only 30% of the PSLR stations reporting had Spanish surnamed sales management.

Engineering. Chief engineers are responsible for the staff maintaining the transmitter and other technical equipment of the radio station. Most stations list this person as chief engineer, engineer or engineering. Thirty-five of the 55 PSLR stations listed information int his category. None reported any Spanish surname engineering department heads.

Programming. Programming directors are responsible for the sound reaching the listeners' ears. They are usually listed as program manager, program director, musical director, or other similar job titles. Thirty-six of the PSLR stations listed information in this category. Twenty-seven listed Spanish surnames and 11 listed non-Spanish surnames. Thus, 75% of the PSLR stations reporting had Spanish surname program directors.

News. News directors are responsible for the newscasts and public affairs programs heard on the station. They are usually listed as news director, newscaster, public affairs director, or other similar job titles. Twenty of the 55 PSLR stations listed information in this category. Fourteen listed Spanish surnames and six listed non-Spanish surnames. Thus, 70% of the PSLR stations reporting had Spanish surnamed news directors.

Promotion. Promotion directors are responsible for maintaining contact with members of the station's audience and with the public in general. They often serve as outside representatives for the stations, attending community functions, and doing limited public affairs programming. Personnel heading these departments are usually called promotion director or promotions. Six of the 55 PSLR stations listed information in this category. Of these, five listed Spanish surnames and one listed a non-Spanish surname. Thus, 83% of the PSLR stations reporting had Spanish surnamed promotion department heads.

Summary of Employment Characteristics. Although the data available in the *Broadcasting Yearbook* are limited, they do provide an overall profile of management on PSLR stations. The profile reported by the data reveals some of the characteristics of a dual labor market in which different ethnic groups have easier access to different levels of employment. In this case the percentage of Spanish surname management increases steadily as the job categories move from internal functions to jobs requiring contact with the audience. Thus, a predominance of non-Spanish surnames was revealed in owner/president, top management, sales and engineering categories; jobs requiring relatively less direct contact with the audience of Spanish-language radio stations.

But Spanish surnames predominated in programming, news and promotion; jobs requiring heavy use of Spanish and ability to relate to the intended audience.

Decision of Findings

The results of the individual sections of the national census of Spanish-language radio are summarized at the end of sections. The purpose of this section is to discuss the implications of those findings as they reveal significant characteristics of Spanish-language radio in the United States.

The national survey indicated that Spanish-language radio continues to be a strong component of broadcasting in the United States, although most stations offer Spanish only a few hours a week and there is a good deal of competition from Mexican border stations. The geographic distribution of Spanish-language stations revealed a wide dispersal with highest concentrations of primarily Spanish stations in states and metropolitan areas with large Latino populations.

The stations' technical characteristics indicated Spanish language programming is most likely to be found on stations on the AM band and commercial stations. The data also revealed that the primary Spanish stations were in less desirable categories when compared to primary English stations in number of broadcast hours and broadcast service class.

The network characteristics of Spanish-language radio stations were found to be primarily affiliations with national sales representation agencies, rather than programming networks. Thus, the networks function primarily as vehicles to facilitate the placement of national advertising on the stations, not as providers of programming or news to the stations. The networks reported link the stations with a central representative, rather than with each other.

In terms of programming, the survey revealed that Spanish is heard on stations offering different types of primary formats, but is infrequently heard on stations with block or variety programming. Spanish is the only specialized program on about a third of the stations surveyed and one of two specialized programs on another 26%. It was also shown that 70% of those stations offering Spanish do so for nine hours or less per week and only 11% of the 485 stations program Spanish as their primary format. Thus, Spanish is most often heard on stations that are primarily programmed for a non-Latino audience and that broadcast Spanish only a few hours a week.

The analysis of management employment indicated a top heavy representation of non-Spanish surnames in ownership, top management, sales and engineering heads and a commensurate heavy representation of Spanish surnames heading programming, news and promotions. Thus, it appeared that a dual labor market may exist in which Anglos hold the dominant positions on primary Spanish-language stations at the upper echelons and internal departments and Latinos are allowed to head departments which require facility in Spanish or ability to relate with the Latino audience.

The results of the national census of Spanish-language radio provide a framework for understanding the characteristics of the medium as they are in the mid-1970s. They also pose a series of provocative questions on the effects of these characteristics on station operation. The data in the next chapter are drawn on the findings of the national census and focus on the operational characteristics of primary Spanish-language radio stations in the Southwestern United States.

NOTES

[1]"Media Briefs," *Los Angeles Times*, July 6, 1975, Part VII, p. 5.
[2]"Radio Report," *Television/Radio Age*, November 27, 1972, p. 12.

41

CHAPTER III

Spanish-language Radio in the Southwest: Patterns of Ownership, Employment, and Wealth

This chapter describes the characteristics of primary Spanish-language radio stations in the United States. The data were gathered from *Broadcast Yearbook*, *Spot Radio*, and information on file in the Public Reference Room of the Federal Communications Commission in Washington, D.C. The station characteristics described in this chapter are designed to provide readers with a greater understanding of the location, ownership, employment, and economics of Spanish-language radio in the Southwest.

Distribution of Stations

There are a total of 41 PSLR stations in the Southwest. As can be seen, the concentration of stations roughly parallels the population densities of the various states. PSLR stations are most likely found in

TABLE 1: PSLR Stations by State

State	Number	Percentage of Total Number of PSLRs in the Southwest	Chicano Population of State*	Percentage of Total Chicano Population in the Southwest
Arizona	4	9.8	333,349	05
California	16	39.0	3,101,589	50
Colorado	2	4.8	286,467	05
New Mexico	4	9.8	407,286	07
Texas	15	36.6	2,059,671	33
Total	41	100.0	6,188,362	100

Source: *Current Population Reports,* "Persons of Spanish Origin in the United States," Series P-20, No. 283, U.S. Bureau of the Census, March 1975.

TABLE 2: PSLR Stations by Market Size.

Market Rank (#1=largest Market Size)	Number of PSLR Stations	Percent of Total
1–10	12	29.5
11–20	11	26.5
21–75	9	22.0
76+	9	22.0
Totals	41	100.0

the larger Chicano markets; Los Angeles, San Antonio, and San Francisco have the highest concentration of stations per city. Nevertheless, nine stations are located in markets too small to be ranked, perhaps indicating a continued service, by radio, to rural areas with fewer listeners.

Extent of Radio Programming in Spanish

As the following table indicates, PSLRs broadcast all, or nearly all, of their time in Spanish, indicating that there is a real difference between "Primary" and "Secondary" Spanish Language Radio. Thus PSLR is composed of stations that broadcast in English, only incidentally. Separate stations vary considerably in absolute time broadcast. The type of license allocated by the FCC and the personal preference of the ownership greatly affect broadcast times, so that the range of hours, per station, devoted to Spanish language programming may vary from 44 hours per week, to 168 hours per week.[1]

Market Power

Advertising rate, the cost of buying one minute of broadcast time on a station, represents the actual market power of the station since it is the only measure of what price the station's time brings on the open

TABLE 3: Percent of Time PSLR Stations Broadcast in Spanish

Percent of Time Broadcast in Spanish	Number of Stations	Percent of Total Stations
50– 75	7	17
76– 90	0	0
91–100	34	83
Totals	41	100

market. Furthermore, advertising rate is an important indicator of power because it represents size of audience and infers the relative influence of the station's messages.

In comparison with its English language counterpart, Spanish language radio draws lower advertising rates. Table 4 shows a few stations holding powerful market positions, with the remainder at relatively weak levels. Seventy-nine percent of all PSLR stations have an advertising rate of $15 or less.

Another measure of market power is found in total assets. Total assets represents the assessed value of the station itself, and is equal to owner's equity plus liabilities. It is the theoretical value that the station would bring if it were sold at the time that the assets were accounted. In this sense, total assets provides a rough outline of the comparative value of the station.[2]

Most PSLR stations (75%) have total assets of less than, or equal to, $300,000. The bulk of PSLR stations contain very modest total assets and advertising rates, while a few stations appear to have much greater total assets and command very high advertising rates. These few stations form a nucleus of power that dominates Spanish language radio.

TABLE 4: Advertising Rates of PSLR Stations

Advertising Rate Per Minute	Number of PSLR Stations	Percent of Total
0– 5 dollars	6	15
6–10 dollars	15	37
11–15 dollars	11	27
16–20 dollars	3	7
21–25 dollars	2	5
25+ dollars	4	9
Totals	41	100

TABLE 5: Total Assets of PSLR Stations

Total Assets	Number of PSLR Stations	Percent of Total
$ 0–$ 100,000	12	32
$ 100,000–$ 500,000	20	53
$ 500,000–$1,000,000	4	10
$1,000,000–$2,000,000	2	5
Totals (3 stations not reporting)	38	100

In addition, PSLR is generally an AM medium that has succeeded in penetrating those communities with high Chicano representation. It is a medium of many small stations with a few very large ones, these large stations exerting enormous market power when compared to their smaller counterparts.

The following sections examine wealth, a key variable in the study of concentration of power, as a function of ownership and employment.

PSLR Wealth and Ownership

Certain indirect measures of wealth and wealth transferral were taken. Wealth was measured as a function of ownership and as a function of employment.

Owner Ethnic Identity

It was assumed that the ethnic identity of the owner was the best available measure of the community in which the owner resides, thereby contributing to the capital base of his/her resident community. Thus, ethnic identity of the owner is used here as a key to understanding PSLR station wealth, and community wealth resulting from PSLR station wealth. Ethnic identity is, furthermore, a measure of differential distribution of ownership. This differential distribution of ownership is a key to the relative wealth levels of the Anglo and Chicano communities.

Owners were identified by surname as the most convenient measure of ethnic identity. Ten owners (24%) were identified with Spanish surnames, and 31 owners (76%) were identified with Anglo surnames. Although it is fairly clear from this initial observation that there is indeed differential distribution of ownership according to ethnic identity, the issue of relative wealth allocation between the two communities is not so clear.

This first measure, though revealing, is also superficial. The complexity of wealth extends beyond the computation of simple ownership ratios. For this reason, total station assets and advertising rates were also measured as a function of owner ethnic identity.

Total Station Assets as a Function of Ownership

Total assets of Spanish-surnamed owned stations equal $1,639,469, while total assets of Anglo owned stations equal $10,064,517. Eight Anglo owned stations control 64% ($6,419,016) of the sum total assets of all Anglo owned stations, and control 55% of all PSLR total assets. In terms of assets, Anglo owned stations accrue a much greater amount of wealth than do their Spanish-surnamed counterparts; additionally, a small core of Anglo owned stations has achieved a dominant position within the PSLR system.

If one refers to the graph (see Chart 1) that illustrates total assets as a function of ownership, one clearly sees the tail on the distribution of Anglo owned stations. When one concentrates on the stations with fewer total assets, there is a rough parallel between the Spanish-surnamed owners and the Anglo owners. Beyond $500,000 in total assets, there are no Spanish-surnamed owned stations. The wealth of this group is better understood when compared with the first quartile of stations—the quartile with the greatest Spanish-surnamed repre-sentation—all of whom have less than $80,000 in total assets per station. In contrast, there are two Anglo owned stations with total assets over 1 million, one with assets over 1.6 million.

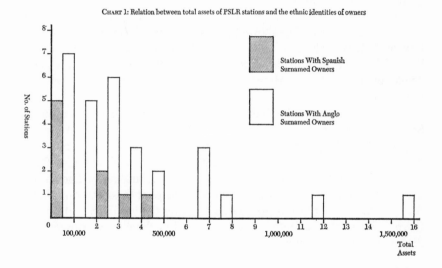

CHART 1: Relation between total assets of PSLR stations and the ethnic identities of owners

That 84% of the total assets of PSLR is controlled by Anglo owners indicates Anglo domination of PSLR. Furthermore, the proportion of total assets controlled by Anglo owners is greater than the numerical proportion of Anglo owners (76%). When total assets is linked to differential distribution of ownership by ethnic identity, it is apparent that wealth is influenced by unequal ethnic representation in PSLR ownership. To further examine this linkage, advertising was studied.

Advertising Rate as a Function of Ownership

The six highest advertising rates of the Spanish surnamed owned stations fall between $7 and $15 per minute, while the six highest advertising rates of the Anglo owned stations fall between $21 and $50 per minute—the three highest being $42, $45, and $50. As in the case of total assets, Anglo owned stations dominate PSLR by virtue of their higher advertising rates.

A reference to the graph (see Chart 2) on advertising rate as a function of ethnic ownership shows the significance of the actual distribution of PSLRs. Below an advertising rate of $15 per minute, there is little difference in the distribution of Spanish-surnamed owned and Anglo owned stations. Above $15 per minute, there is no Spanish-surnamed representation.

Both total assets and advertising rate indicate a concentration of Spanish owned stations at the lower end of the range. Anglo owned stations, though also represented at the lower end of the range, exclusively dominate the upper end. Eight Anglo owned stations (25%) control 55% of total assets and 45% of total advertising rates. The strong market position disclosed by the advertising rates of these stations places Anglo owners in a position solidly dominating the industry. Not only is there differential distribution of ownership, but there is an even greater disparity in market power.

PSLR Owners' Additional Properties

Because the wealth of any industry does not exist in a vacuum, there is a need for the examination of wealth as part of its larger social context. In order to better understand the systemic ties between PSLR and the rest of the economy, it was necessary to investigate the interconnections of ownership between this medium and other sectors of the economy.

For the purposes of this study, an owner's "aditional properties" refers to the properties, in addition to the station, which the station

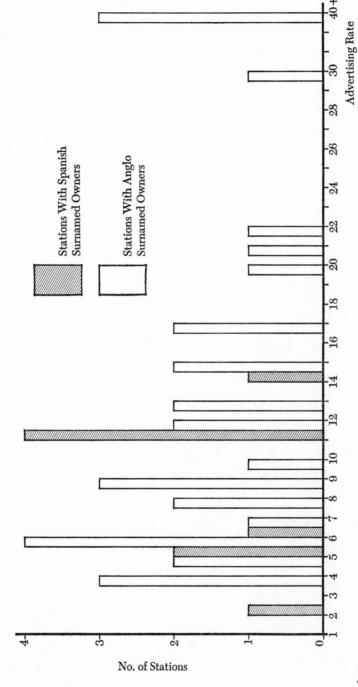

CHART 2: Relation between advertising rates of PSLR stations and ethnic identities of owners

Stations With Spanish
Surnamed Owners

Stations With Anglo
Surnamed Owners

No. of Stations

Advertising Rate

49

owner owns, or in which he/she has a major interest. "Additional properties" were divided into "broadcast properties" (e.g. cable outlets, television stations, radio stations) and "non broadcast properties" (e.g. movie theaters, cemeteries, used car lots).

Additional "Broadcast Properties"

There are 12 Anglo station owners with a greater number of broadcast properties than any Spanish-surnamed owner. Out of 81 additional broadcast properties held by all owners, Anglo owners hold 76 (94%). There is only one case of a Spanish-surnamed owner with 3 additional broadcast properties, while there are 4 cases of Anglo station owners with 10 or more additional broadcast properties. In this instance the disparity in ownership patterns is distinct. There is a clear concentration of ownership in the hands of a few persons (men), all of whom are Anglos.

Apparently, media domination by Anglo station owners extends beyond the confines of Spanish language radio. It is an important aspect of systemic inequality because it establishes the possibility of similar Anglo influence in other areas of broadcasting.

Additional "Nonbroadcast Properties"

It appears that many station owners, of both ethnic backgrounds, are entrepreneurs in the nonbroadcast area. PSLR station owners hold 61 additional nonbroadcast properties. Seven Anglo station owners hold three or more nonbroadcast properties, while only three Spanish-surnamed owners hold three or more nonbroadcast properties. Of the total number of nonbroadcast properties held by all owners, Anglo owners hold 46 (75%) and Spanish-surnamed owners hold 15 (28%). Unlike the distribution of broadcast properties, the distribution of nonbroadcast properties parallels the numerical distribution of Anglo and Spanish-surnamed owners. However, three Anglo owners own 25 (41%) of all additional nonbroadcast properties, indicating continued concentration of wealth in the hands of a few Anglos.

In summary, Anglo station owners hold 121 (86%) of the 142 identified additional properties, while nine Anglo owners (29% of all owners) hold more additional properties than any Spanish-surnamed owner, thus indicating significant unequal distribution of both broadcast and nonbroadcast properties. Seven Anglo station owners hold 74 (52%) additional properties, further indicating an unequal distribution of wealth. The measures of additional properties as a function of ethnic ownership, corroborates the patterns of differential wealth distribution found in the ownership data. Clearly, the unequal distribution of

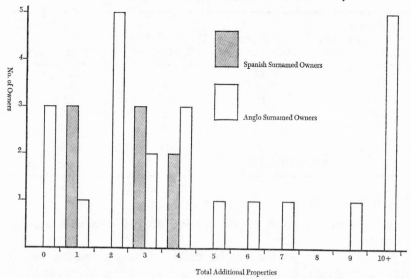

wealth is not an isolated phenomenon, but extends beyond the confines of commercial broadcasting.

Using each of the six measures of wealth and ownership, strong evidence was found to verify the existence of an unequal distribution of wealth between Anglo and Chicano owners. Advertising rate and total assets, as particularly strong indirect measures of PSLR wealth, indicate that wealth is generated from the Chicano audience and redistributed to the Anglo community. Anglo station owners, especially a few large and powerful station owners, own more stations, control more assets, command higher advertising rates, and have more additional property holdings than anyone else. The wealth of these Anglo owners is generated from the Spanish-speaking community, through the medium of commercial Spanish language radio.

Examining PSLR wealth as a function of ownership is only a part, albeit a critical and complex part, of the issue of PSLR wealth. A second part of this study examines differential distributions of several levels of personnel in Spanish-language radio.

PSLR Wealth and Personnel

In further analysis of PSLR wealth distribution, a second stage of the study was conducted examining wealth distribution through personnel.

51

Percent of Management with Spanish Surnames	Number of PSLR Stations	Percent of Total PSLR Stations	Anglo Owned/ Spanish Surname Owned (A/Ss)
0	13	34	13/0 (A/Ss)
1 – 25	3	8	3/0
26– 50	17	45	12/5
51– 75	2	5	1/1
76–100	3	8	0/3
Totals	38	100	29/9
(3 stations not reporting)			

Management with Spanish Surnames

Stations were arrayed by the percent of managers with Spanish surnames.

Management teams tend to be small, with most stations having three people listed as managers (total number of managers for all 38 stations reporting = 109). Yet even with this consideration, it is noteworthy that there are so few Spanish-surnamed managers (total number of Spanish-surnamed managers = 34, or 31% of all PSLR managers). Only five stations (13%) have management teams where Spanish-surnamed managers are in the majority. Of these five stations, four have Spanish-surnamed owners; only one Anglo owned station has a primarily Spanish-surnamed management team. But even stations with Spanish-surnamed owners do not have strong Spanish-surname representation; five of the nine Spanish-surnamed owned stations reporting, have Spanish-surnamed managers in the minority, although all Spanish-surnamed owned stations have at least one Spanish-surnamed manager. By contrast, fully one third of all PSLR stations have no Spanish-surnamed managers at all.

Thus in examining the question of differential wealth distribution, it is apparent that more Anglo managers than Spanish-surnamed managers are drawing wealth from their association with PSLR. If less than a third (31%) are Spanish surnamed, and if salaries between Anglo and Spanish-surnamed managers are equal (perhaps open to question), then over two thirds of the wealth from management salaries does not return to the community that generated it, but instead is redistributed to the Anglo community. What wealth is derived from PSLR as a function of management activities is unequally distributed.

In addition, the existence of 13 Anglo owned stations with no Spanish-surnamed managers raises serious questions as to the quality of decisions made regarding Spanish language formats, and the Spanish speaking audience. Without a single Spanish-surnamed person in a decision making position, isolation between the station and its audience seems likely to occur.

Engineers with Spanish Surnames

The chief engineer requires FCC certification of his/her skills and is responsible for the technical operation of the station. The rigorous requirements for the position, and the necessary certification, present an interesting test of Spanish-surnamed employee penetration into the station hierarchy.

Of all the stations reporting (40), only one station (also Spanish-surnamed owned) had a Spanish-surnamed chief engineer. It is significant that this, a highly skilled position requiring specific certification, had the least Spanish-surnamed penetration of any of the identified station positions. This category offers the strongest evidence of differential distribution of personnel, and, by inference, the strongest evidence of unequal wealth distribution.

Employess with Spanish Surnames

Twenty-eight stations reporting six or more employees (other than management or engineering personnel) were catalogued by the ethnicity of their employees.

In contrast to Spanish-surnamed managers and engineers, the number of stations reporting a high percentage of Spanish-surnamed personnel is large, since most stations operate with 8–15 employees. Of a total of 417 PSLR employees reported, 268 (64%) were Spanish sur-

TABLE 7: PSLR Employees with Spanish Surnames

Percent of Employees with Spanish Surnames	Number of PSLR Stations	Percent of Total Stations Reporting	Anglo Owned/ Spanish Surname Owned (A/Ss)
0 – 25	0	0	0/0 (A/Ss)
26– 50	6	21	5/1
51– 75	8	29	8/0
76–100	14	50	10/4
Totals	28	100	23/5
(13 stations not reporting)			

53

named. One explanation for this finding is the station need for personnel fluent in Spanish. It would seem that news persons, announcers, and receptionists speaking fluent Spanish are a large percent of the above figures.

An interesting aspect of this finding, and the only anecdotal information available, is the case of station KOFY, a San Francisco Bay area PSLR station. KOFY reports 25 non-managerial or engineering employees—10 full-time and 14 part-time. KOFY also reports 16 Spanish-surnamed employees in this group of 24. Of the 16 Spanish-surnamed employees, 13 of them are part-time. Of the 8 Anglo employees, only one is part-time. Thus an apparent Spanish-surnamed majority is questionable when closely examined. In this case, it would seem that Spanish-surnamed employees hold the least secure, and possibly least lucrative positions. One is, therefore, cautioned against accepting employee data as definitely indicating greater wealth accrual on the part of Spanish-surnamed employees.

In reviewing the findings on PSLR personnel, strong evidence was found to verify the existence of differential distribution between Anglo and Spanish-surnamed personnel. In the two most lucrative personnel categories (manager and chief engineer), Spanish-surnamed people were in an extreme minority, Anglo personnel accruing the greater portion of the wealth generated from these two positions. In the third personnel category, Spanish-surnamed employees were in the majority. However, this is the personnel category which generates the least amount of wealth per capita and, therefore, indicates a continued unequal distribution of income as a result of PSLR employment. Moreover, the case of KOFY cautions that Spanish-surnamed employees might still be at disadvantage within this last category as well.

Summary

Differential distribution by ethnicity exists at numerous levels of ownership and employment in PSLR. Unequal representation was was found among owners, managers, and chief engineers. In the lowest employment category, that of general employee, there was a substantial representation of Spanish-surnamed individuals.

Personal wealth derived from participation in PSLR was found to be distributed by ethnicity. Anglo ownership of the wealthiest and most powerful stations indicates that profits from those stations are accrued by Anglo owners, and therefore, by the Anglo community. Moreover, Anglo owners also hold far more numerous additional properties than their Spanish-surnamed counterparts, thus enhancing Anglo wealth and influence within the Spanish language radio industry. By contrast, Spanish-surnamed owners having the smallest and poorest stations, draw only a small portion of the profits generated by the Spanish language radio industry.

The over-representation of Anglo managers, and the over-representation of Anglo managers in the wealthier stations, further indicates differential distribution of personal wealth. Another profitable category of PSLR employment, that of chief engineer, showed a near complete absence of Spanish-surnamed representation. Only in the general employee category could it be inferred that Spanish-surnamed personnel were drawing a significantly greater portion of the wealth generated at that level, and even here it was questionable. It is clear that there is a differential distribution of personal wealth as a result of PSLR activities.

Differential distribution of influence was inferred from evidence of differential access to the more powerful positions within PSLR. A few Anglo owners occupy the strongest market positions by owning the biggest stations and by holding more additional properties than anyone else. This places them in a position to exercise more power in the marketplace than those owners with smaller stations and fewer additional properties.

Similarly, fewer Spanish-surnamed individuals have access to positions in management and engineering. Moreover, Spanish-surnamed individuals are almost totally excluded from the larger, more powerful stations. What influence and power there is, is effectively out of the hands of Chicanos.

The integration of PSLR with the community it is intended to serve is questionable because of the differential distribution of personnel, wealth and, by inference, influence. Spanish-language radio is an industry whose sole cause for existence is to communicate with the Spanish-speaking listener. Yet, ironically, it has a relatively low penetration of Spanish-surnamed individuals into its decision-making levels. It is inferred in this study that those Anglo individuals who are at decision-making levels are not likely to be members of the Chicano, or Spanish speaking community. It, therefore, appears that the possibility of the community to influence the programming or conduct of PSLR, is quite likely impaired by this separation of ownership and listenership.

Anglo owners of PSLR stations were also found to own more additional properties in media, and non media, related industries, thus raising the issue of differential distribution of wealth, and influence in industries other than PSLR. Linkages, through ownership, with other broadcast properties were quite high and largely dominated by a few Anglo owners. Linkages with nonbroadcast properties were more evenly distributed between Spanish-surnamed and Anglo owners, but still dominated by a few Anglo owners. This evidence of strong integration between PSLR and other industries does not establish that patterns of differential distribution exist in other industries, nor does it establish that patterns of differential distribution exist across industries. It does raise the possibility of such patterns, and so opens the question for future investigation.

NOTES

[1]Of the stations in the 50–75% group, two stations—KBRG-FM and KPIP-FM— broadcast most of their non-Spanish time in some other non-English language.

[2]Pyle, William W. and White, John A., *Fundamental Accounting Principles*; Richard D. Irwin, Inc., Homewood, Ill., 1966, p. 57–59.

CHAPTER IV

*Comparison of News and Public Affairs Betweeen a Spanish-
and an English-language Station*

Although the ownership and employment characteristics of Spanish-language radio discussed in the previous chapter provide important institutional information on the structure and makeup of PSLR, no analysis of any broadcast media would be complete without addressing content. The purpose of this chapter is to comparatively study public service programming on Primary English Language Radio (PELR) and Primary Spanish Language Radio (PSLR). Public service programming (news broadcasts and public service announcements) was selected as indicative of a station's provision of important information to its audience. Entertainment programming is not considered in this monograph because of its low informational content and difficulty of analysis.

While it would have been impossible to systematically analyze news and PSA content on all 41 PSLRs, the choice of two case study stations provided a practical solution to the problem of studying content. PSLR station KCOR, and PELR station KONO were chosen as the case study subjects. Both KCOR and KONO broacast a middle of the road entertainment format aimed at listeners over 18 years of age. KCOR consistently ranked second among all radio stations in San Antonio, Texas and first among Spanish language radio stations; during this same period, KONO consistently ranked between fifth and eighth among all radio stations in San Antonio.[1] Both radio stations have a reputation for community service and responsiveness; in particular, KCOR has a reputation for extraordinary community rapport. San Antonio, Texas was chosen as the site for the case studies because of its large Chicano population.[2]

TABLE 1:   Frequency of Local News Items and Non-Local News Items
on KONO and KCOR

Type of News Item	KONO (PELR)	Percent of Total	KCOR (PSLR)	Percent of Total
Local News Items	101	44	82	52
Non-Local News Items	131	66	76	48
Total News Items	232	100	158	100

*Information a a Function of News on PELR Station
KONO, and on PSLR Station KCOR*

A content analysis of news broadcasts on the two stations in San
Antonio, Texas was conducted in December 1975. Both stations were
simultaneously recorded, three times a day, during a seven-day period.

Total news broadcasts were divided into local news items and non-
local news items. In this content analysis, a news item was defined as
"local" if specific reference was made to either San Antonio, Texas, or
Bexar County.

The above findings indicate that KONO provided more local news
items, more non-local news items, and thus more total news items to its
San Antonio audience. Indeed, KONO broadcast 20% more local news
items than did KCOR, and 32% more total news items. KCOR did allo-
cate a larger portion of its total news to local news items; 52% of
KCOR's news items were local versus 44% local news items for KONO.
But KCOR still broadcast fewer local news items.

However, before claiming that the Spanish speaking listener received
less information than the English speaking listener, it was necessary to
further reexamine the news broadcasts as a function of time. Whereas
the first findings measured the *number* of news items broadcast over

TABLE 2:   Amount of Time Devoted to Local News and Non-Local News
on KONO and KCOR (Time is in seconds)

	KONO (PELR)	Percent of Total	KCOR (PSLR)	Percent of Total
Local News	2838 (47:18)	53	2360 (39:20)	58
Non-Local News	2542 (42:22)	47	1738 (28:58)	42
Total News	5380 (89:40) (1:29:40)	100	4098 (68:18) (1:08:18)	100

KONO and KCOR, the second set of findings measures the *amount of time* devoted to news in order to determine whether one audience received fewer minutes of local broadcast news.

The data on amount of time devoted to news broadcasts indicates that KONO devoted more time to local, non-local, and total news than KCOR. In both stations, local news was longer in duration than non-local news. However, KONO broadcast 47 minutes, 18 seconds of local news time, as opposed to KCOR's 39 minutes, 20 seconds of local news time, even though KCOR allocated 58% of its time to local news and KONO allocated 53% of its time to local news. Clearly the English speaking audience listening to KONO received more local news.

To make inferences on the basis of this data, however, would be fallacious, since only news *quantity* has so far been examined. In order to make some form of judgment on the comparative levels of information acquisition between Anglos and Chicanos, one would also have to have complementary information on the *quality* of news. The second set of data examines news content in an effort to determine information quality.

Only local news and total news content were analyzed for information quality, since it was felt that these categories would be the most salient in determining the usefulness of information available to each audience. Local news content was divided into three major subject categories: "government," "crime," and "other." No other specific subject categories appeared in sufficient frequency to be measured (KONO, for example, carried only five sports items during the seven day period of content analysis). The "other" category varied in subject matter from straight news (e.g., an automobile accident at a new shopping mall) to feature items (e.g., Laurelio and Norma Morales became the proud parents of their 14th child on Dec. 9, 1975). The shades between straight and featured news were considered too fine to attempt a division within the category.

TABLE 3: Frequency of Local News Items by Subject on KONO and KCOR

Local News Items	KONO (PELR)	Percent of Total	KCOR (PSLR)	Percent of Total
Government	44	44	29	35
Crime	9	9	24	29
Other	47	47	27	33
Unspecified	1	1	2	3
Totals	101	100	82	100

Both stations devoted more local news items to government than any other single subject. Though some of these news stories cover federal and state government as well as city/county government, they are considered local by virtue of having taken place in San Antonio/Bexar County.

Most interesting in this set of data was the relative frequency of news items on the subject of local crime. KCOR clearly reported more local crime stories than KONO. While both stations reported such major crimes as homocides and possession of drugs in large amounts, KCOR also reported car thefts, burglaries, and family quarrels, often giving the names and addresses of those involved. It is hard to say whether this attraction to minor crimes represents a conscious effort at sensationalism on the part of KCOR's management. What is clear is that the broadcasting of minor crimes by KCOR limited KCOR's available time for news items on other, perhaps more valuable, subjects. KCOR, with a smaller amount of news items than KONO, chose to devote 30% of its news items to crime subjects, as opposed to 9% for KONO.

These findings indicate that the English-speaking audience received more information on local subjects than the Spanish-speaking audience. Moreover, this advantage on the part of the English-speaking audience was extended even further by KCOR's use of limited air time to report on minor crimes, thus limiting the Spanish-speaking audience's exposure to local news on other subjects.

When total news content was examined, the data were found to parallel the findings for local news. Here again, KONO broadcast more total news items in the subject areas of "government" and "other," while KCOR broadcast more total news items on "crime." Chicanos listening to KCOR did not receive the same amount of information that Anglos did by listening to KONO, in any subject area except crime. Nor was the information comparable, since KCOR relied heavily on stories of minor crime.

TABLE 4:   Frequency of Total News Items by Subject on KONO and KCOR

Total News Item	KONO (PELR)	Percent of Total	KCOR (PSLR)	Percent of Total
Government	106	46	54	35
Crime	33	14	45	29
Other	92	40	57	36
Unspecified	1	0	2	0
Totals	231	100	156	100

A review of the content analysis of news broadcasts show the following results:

1) Listeners of KONO (PELR) received more local news, by item, than did listeners of KCOR (PSLR). KONO broadcast 20% more local news items than did KCOR.

2) KONO devoted more news time to local news than did KCOR.

3) KONO broadcast more total news, both local and non-local, than did KCOR, KONO broadcasting 32% more total news items than KCOR.

4) KONO offered more news in every subject category except crime. KCOR's listeners received only half the government news that KONO's listeners received. KCOR allocated a high portion of its space and time to minor crime (31%) emphasizing sensational aspects of the crimes reported.

By nearly every measure employed, KONO provided more local news to its audience than did KCOR. Listeners of KONO clearly received more information specifically related to their community than did the listeners of KCOR. The findings indicate that a relationship of unequal information flow exists between the Anglo community and the Chicano community in San Antonio, Texas. What is clear, is that English speaking listeners of KONO are receiving more information about their immediate environment than are the Spanish speaking listeners of KCOR.

Community Support Through Public Service
Announcements (PSAs) on KONO and KCOR

A content analysis of PSAs on KONO and KCOR was conducted concurrently with the content analysis of news broadcasts. Data were gathered from each station's PSA files, representing all PSAs over a three year period.

PSAs were divided into locally and non-locally sponsored announcements. While local PSAs broadcast by KONO were in the majority (70%), local PSAs broadcast by KCOR were in the minority (39%), KONO also airing a greater number of total PSAs than KCOR. The

TABLE 5: *Frequency of Locally and Non-Locally Sponsored*
PSAs on KONO and KCOR

Number of PSAs	KONO (PELR)	Percent of Total	KCOR (PSLR)	Percent of Total
Local PSAs	144	70	37	39
Non-Local PSAs	60	30	57	61
Total PSAs	204	100	94	100

indication in this first set of findings is that local community access, through PSAs, on KCOR, was very limited. It would seem that the channel of Public Service Announcements was being utilized by organizations other than the local community organizations for which it was intended. However, the category of "local" versus "non-local" gives only partial information. One is also interested in determining whether a "local" PSA is sponsored by an organization in the Chicano community or in the Anglo community.

In order to determine whether sponsors of PSAs were from the Chicano community or from the Anglo community, the somewhat deficient method of identifying sponsoring organizations by census tract was utilized. This method was not as biased as it might have been, since San Antonio is still a relatively segregated city. Local PSAs were, therefore, listed by census tracts as a function of the ethnicity of those tracts.

It would seem that there is little local community access, for PSAs, on KCOR. Not only was the PSA channel on KCOR dominated by non-local organizations, but it was also dominated by local organizations from the Anglo community. Local organizations from the Chicano community formed the smallest category of sponsors on KCOR. Anglo community domination of PSAs is a particularly important finding, since PSAs are the only channel of radio access for non-commercial organizations.

The previous data has shown Anglo domination of the PSA channel on both KONO and KCOR, but has not shown which types of organi-

TABLE 7: Frequency of PSAs by Type of Sponsoring
Organization on KONO and KCOR

Type of Sponsoring Organization, Local PSAs	KONO (PELR)	Percent of Total	KCOR (PSLR)	Percent of Total
Government	27	19	19	51
Private	117	81	18	49
	144	100	37	100
Non-Local PSAs				
Government	19	32	34	61
Private	40	68	22	39
	59	100	56	100
Total PSAs				
Government	46	23	53	57
Private	157	77	40	43
	203	100	93	100

zations are actually using the PSA channel. In order to determine this, sponsoring organizations were identified as either belonging in the government sector or the private sector.

The single largest sponsoring group on KONO was the group composed of local private organizations, while the single largest sponsoring group on KCOR was the group composed of non-local government organizations. In both local and non-local PSAs, the private sector is the largest sponsor of PSAs on KONO, but the smallest sponsor of PSAs on KCOR.

The data in this set of findings indicates that the PSA channel is functioning differently for both stations. On KONO, PSAs appear to be a channel for local private community organizations to gain access to radio broadcasting. On KCOR, PSAs appear to be a channel for non-community organizations, in particular government, to funnel their messages into the Spanish speaking community. Local private Chicano community organizations have the least access to PSAs on KCOR of any of the identified groups; PSAs on KCOR appear to form a direct open channel, rather than a loop as on KONO.

A review of the content analysis of PSAs indicates:

1) 70% of PSAs on KONO were sponsored by local organizations. In contrast, only 39% of PSAs broadcast by KCOR were sponsored by local organizations.

2) 56% of KONO's PSAs were sponsored by organizations in Anglo census tracts, while only 32% of KCOR's PSAs were sponsored by organizations in Chicano census tracts. In addition, KONO drew more PSAs from Chicano tracts (45) than KCOR did (12).

3) 58% of all PSAs on KONO came from local private organizations supporting an interpretation of local community support of the PSA channel on KONO. 57% of all PSAs on KCOR came from government sponsors reinforcing an interpretation of government support of the PSA channel on KCOR. Local private sponsors were the smallest single group of PSA sponsors on KCOR.

The findings of the content analysis of PSAs indicate two very different uses of the PSA channel. For PELR and English speaking audiences, PSAs appear to be an effective form of local community voice. For PSLR and Spanish speaking audiences, PSAs appear to be an effective channel for government and non-Chicano community messages.

Summary

It is evident from the content analysis of news broadcasts that English speaking listeners are provided with more information on which to base decisions about their immediate environment. In number of news items devoted to local news and in amount of time devoted to local news, PELR station KONO provided more local news than did PSLR station KCOR. KONO also provided more information in most subject areas, particularly in the area of local government. Only in the area of local crime did KCOR provide more information. By default, Spanish speaking listeners were left at a potential disadvantage vis-à-vis their English speaking counterparts. Thus, the Anglo community, from which most English speaking listeners come, was at a potential advantage in the utilization of information derived from local news.

This advantage is accentuated because of the limited nature of Spanish language media. San Antonio, the case study community, has three Spanish language radio stations and one Spanish language television station; it has no Spanish language daily newspaper. By contrast, San Antonio has twenty radio stations, four television stations and two daily newspapers in English. Nevertheless, the Chicano community of San Antonio is in a favorable position when compared to most Spanish speaking communities in other cities, which are usually limited to one PSLR station with no other media. Whereas KONO is one of many sources of information for the English speaking listener, KCOR is virtually the only source of information for the Spanish speaking listener. Between the two is a significant information gap.

Findings from the content analysis of Public Service Announcements indicate that the PSA channel works differently within PELR than it does within PSLR. Whereas PSAs on KONO appear to be an effective public voice for private Anglo community organizations, PSAs on KCOR appear to be a channel for non-community, primarily government, messages.

It is not clear what effect these differences in newsbroadcasting and PSAs have on the respective audiences. We know so little about media effects on Spanish speaking audiences, that it is difficult to hypothesize as to what uses the Spanish speaking audience might be making of this type of information.[3] While it is clear that the media environment of the Spanish speaking listener is much sparser than the media environment of the English speaking listener, how this affects the utilization of broadcast information by the media consumer can only be inferred.

The differences in informational content between KONO and KCOR do raise the question of an information gap between the English speaking audience and the Spanish speaking audience. Whether each community makes efficient use of the broadcast information available to it, is debatable. What is not debatable is that the English speaking community has a greater wealth of information to draw on and, thus, is potentially able to make greater use of the information available to it. Only a better understanding of the communication effects on the two communities can indicate the impact of this information gap.

Finally, one must question the quality of news broadcasting and PSAs on stations of lesser stature than KCOR. KCOR has one of the largest news staffs among PSLRs[4] One can only surmise that some PSLRs are providing news information of considerably less quality, perhaps widening the information gap in some communities. Indeed, there is no indication that KCOR is not doing the best one could expect under the circumstances that it operates under. Nor is there any indication that either KONO or KCOR are operating against FCC regulations. Yet the media and market conditions of San Antonio are such that the case for an information gap with its potential negative effects on the Spanish speaking audience is plausible.

NOTES

[1]Both stations supplied ratings data from Arbitron Radio research bureau. Ratings were established during the October/November rating period.

[2]*Census of Population: General Social and Economic Characteristics for Texas,* PC (1)–C45, 1970. Persons of Spanish Origin in San Antonio = 52%. This is probably an undercount, but roughly idicates the size of San Antonio's population of Spanish origin.

[3]Schement, Jorge Reina, "Literature on the Chicano Audience in Review," pp 119–124, in *Aztlan,* Vol. 7, No. 1, Spring 1978.

[4]KCOR has 8 news employees; three of them are fulltime. KCOR ranks second among American PSLRs in total news employees. This information was gathered from station renewal applications on file at the Federal Communications Commission.

CHAPTER V

Case Study of Spanish-language Radio Station XXX

Spanish-language radio station XXX is located in a major metropolitan area of the Southwestern United States and is one of several Spanish-language broadcast stations in the area. The station now broadcasts full time in Spanish, having started experimenting with part time Spanish programming in the 1940s. The early programming was produced by Latino program brokers who bought the air time at a block rate from the station, programmed their own show, and sold the advertising for their time. The difference between what they paid the station and took in from the advertisers was their own profit or loss.

Early Spanish-language programs on the station were usually aired in the early morning and just before signoff, with the prime day segments reserved for English-language programs. In the early 1950s the station began steadily increasing its Spanish-language programming until it became all Spanish. In the process the brokerage system was also eliminated. The brokers were made employees of the station who were paid a salary and a commission for advertising sold or aired on their programs. Thus, the Anglo station management cut itself in for a larger share of the profits as the amount of Spanish-language programming increased.

A former XXX broker who became an employee in this period described how Spanish-language radio had steadily grown:

> Well, little by little it (Spanish-language radio) was growing. Little by little it was increasing itself. Little by little it was having more advertisers. Little by little the stations gave it more importance. The stations saw that it was a real business, then put themselves in charge of selling the commercials. They began to sell more and at a higher price than ours. Because we charged very little and they charged very much more.

Elimination of the brokers allowed the station management to set a flat rate for advertising and ended the undercutting of prices by which the brokers used to compete for advertisers. However, the disc jockeys were allowed to continue selling advertising on their programs and were paid a commission or talent fee for commercials aired on their programs. They also retained the responsibility for the program format and music they played. In this period Spanish-language radio continued to be "personality radio" in which audience identification was promoted around the personalities on the air, not with the station itself.

As the station made the transition from part time Spanish to full time Spanish the commercialization of air time also became more pronounced. In the early part of the 1950s the station's license renewal application to the Federal Communications Commission (FCC) reported that 59% of the station's time was sold commercially and 41% was unsold or sustaining. By the early 1960s, when the station had completed the transition to full time Spanish, the commercial time had increased to 67% and sustaining time decreased to 33%. The trend was also apparent in the station's spot announcements, which went from 43% commercial to 89% commercial in the same period.

At the same time that XXX was becoming more commercialized the programming was also becoming more entertainment oriented. The station's entertainment programs grew from 68% to 85% of the programming during the period it was making the transition to full time Spanish. Most of the entertainment programming was introduced at the expense of religious, educational, discussion and talk programs. Thus, the switch to full time Spanish also witnessed the dislocation of brokers and replacement by an employee arrangement, increased commercialization of time, and growth of entertainment programming at the expense of more balanced formats.

In the 1960s XXX continued to develop by introducing regular newscasts and sharply increasing efforts to attract advertisers. The newscasts were later characterized by the XXX general manager as "a question of force feeding the community at first," since they were apparently an innovation in Spanish-language radio at the time. However, he noted that the listeners would soon call up to complain "if the newscasts were missed or cut short." On the commercial side, the station developed a professional sales force to attract national brand name advertisers to the station, which had earlier depended primarily on local barrio businesses for advertising. Between the late 1950s and late 1960s advertising billings increased from $12,000 to $80,000 a month.

In the 1960s, the management changed XXX from "personality" programming to format radio. This involved severing the former brokers from the station, separating sales and programming functions, and introducing a station format sound that was consistent throughout the broadcast day and did not vary from disc jockey to disc jockey. Thus, XXX sought to develop listener loyalty to the station, rather than to the personalities. It did this by introducing a consistent music format that would attract the younger listeners desired by advertisers and minimizing the role of the disc jockeys as personalities.

The current owner of XXX is an Anglo licensee of a number of other broadcast stations that program Spanish and other formats. Although the owner visits the station regularly, the daily operations of XXX are supervised by a bilingual Anglo vice-president and general manager appointed by the owner. The remainder of this chapter is divided between different aspects of station operation during the mid-1970s.

Management and Employment

Radio station XXX operates on a functional distribution of management responsibilities. The owner/president is the licensee of the station and has overall responsibility for XXX and its sister stations. Reporting to the owner/president is the vice president and general manager, who is responsible for the daily operation of the station and supervises the staff. Reporting directly to the vice president and general manager are the various department heads: program director, sales manager, chief engineer, and office manager (see Chart 1).

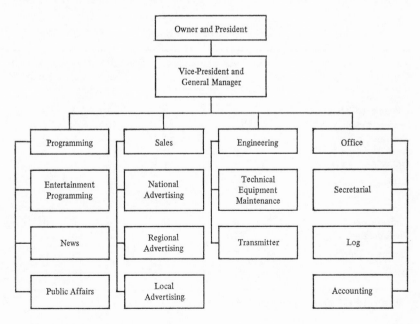

Each department head is responsible for specific functions. Program responsibilities include entertainment, news and public affairs. The sales manager is responsible for national, regional and local advertising. The chief engineer handles maintenance of equipment, monitoring of power during broadcasts, and transmitter operation. Unlike other stations, XXX engineers do not sit in the broadcast booth to handle voice modulation, logging, cartridges and other technical duties. Because of language differences between Spanish-speaking announcers and English-speaking engineers the XXX announcers must handle these jobs themselves. The office manager is responsible for the secretarial pool, receptionist, traffic, maintenance of the log and local accounting.

During the period of information gathering XXX reported 26 full time and seven part time employees. Of these 33 employees, 18 were reported to the FCC as "Spanish-Surnamed Americans" (the agency's designation for Latinos). Of the 18, 15 were full time and three were part time. All of the 18 were found in either the professional jobs (primary announcers and newscasters) or sales. No Latinos were reported in technical or clerical categories and only one was reported in officials/managers. Thus, the Latino employees were concentrated largely in positions in which a Latino's presence would be required or desirable; on-the-air and selling advertising.

An analysis of the station's staff directory revealed the same pattern, with the addition of Latino office workers. The vice president and gen-

TABLE 1: Frequency Distribution of XXX Employess by FCC Form 395

Category	All Employees			Spanish Surnamed Personnel		
	Total	Male	Female	Total	Male	Female
Fulltime:						
Officials to Managers	2	2	0	1	1	0
Professionals	10	8	11	10	9	1
Technicians	5	5	0	0	0	0
Sales Workers	6	6	0	5	5	0
Office and Clerical	4	0	4	0	0	0
Fulltime Totals	27	21	15	16	15	1
Parttime:						
Professionals	3	3	0	3	3	0
Technicians	4	4	0	0	0	0
Parttime Totals	7	7	0	3	3	0
Total	34	28	5	19	18	1

Source: FCC Form Annual Employment Report.

eral manager indicated he was interested in making a concerted effort to hire Latinos as job openings became available and that he was particularly interested in hiring Chicanos raised and educated in the United States. However, biographical information on XXX's Latino employees indicated that the station was heavily dependent on Latinos born, educated, and experienced in broadcasting in Latin America.

For example, all announcers (with the exception of one) were born, educated and received their first broadcasting experience in Latin America. They later migrated to the United States and sought employment in Spanish-language broadcasting. The one exception was a part time university student who was born and partially educated in Mexico before coming to the United States. In a preliminary interview the vice president and general manager and program director said the station relied heavily on announcers from Latin America because it was impossible to find Chicanos who could read and write Spanish fluently. The picture for local Latinos was a little better in sales, where there were two Chicanos who had entered Spanish-language broadcasting in the United States. The office staff also had two Latinos; one who entered Spanish-language broadcasting in the United States and the other with previous broadcast experience in Latin America.

A summary table of the 20 Latino employees listed in the staff directory indicates that 18 (90%) were born in Latin America, 16 (80%) were educated in Latin America, and 14 (70%) received their first broadcast experience in Latin America (see Table 2). Since those 20 constitute

TABLE 2: Frequency Distribution of XXX Latino Employees by Selected Background Characteristics

Job Category	Number of Latinos	Country of Birth		Country of Education			Start in Broadcasting		
		L.A.	U.S.	L.A.	U.S.	Unk.	L.A.	U.S.	Unk.
Top Management	0	0	0	0	0	0	0	0	0
Announcers	14	14	0	12	1	1	12	1	1
Sales	4	2	2	3	1	0	1	3	0
Office Staff	2	2	0	1	1	0	1	1	0
Engineering	0	0	0	0	0	0	0	0	0
Total	20	18	2	16	3	1	14	5	1

Sources: XXX Staff Directory, XXX License Renewal and interviews with XXX personnel.

Key: L.A. = Latin America
U.S. = United States
Unk. = Unknown

two-thirds of the XXX staff, it should be clear that only a small percentage of the station's workforce is comprised of Latinos who were born, educated, and introduced to broadcasting in the United States.

In addition to the underrepresentation of local Latinos, there is also an underrepresentation of women in non-clerical positions. For many years XXX, like many Spanish-language radio stations, had a popular female personality on the air in the morning. But her airtime was reduced to short pre-recorded spots covering recipes, advice to listeners, and tips for women. These spots were aired during the morning hours when a male disc jockey was on the air. Although another woman also taped announcements for the station, there were no women with programs, working as disc jockeys, or reporting the news. When asked about this the program director expressed doubts about the capacity of women to handle the physical aspects of the disc jockey's job. He said:

> In my long years of experience as an announcer, up to this date I have not found a woman who has the same capacity as a man, not mental capacity, but mechanical capacity. Because you have to operate the board and you have to do it in a certain quick manner. The woman has the tendency to put her own feminine touch in what she does, which is natural because of their sex. But, after this, she doesn't have the manual ability to manage the board, or it could be she knows it, but not in the close manner that an announcer ought to be able to do it.

Economics

Like all commercial broadcast media in the United States, XXX generates its revenues by selling advertising spots and program sponsorship on its broadcast time. But the time itself is of no value unless there is an audience the advertiser wants to attract listening to it. The amount of money stations charge advertisers depends on the size and demographic characteristics of the audience their programs attract.

Advertisers are naturally interested in stations drawing audiences that make good consumers. By this indicator Spanish-speaking Latinos would appear to be poor advertising investments. Median family income for Latinos is 25% lower than the national average and 25% of all Latinos live in poverty. Latinos tend to have a higher unemployment rate than the national norm and are underrepresented in the higher income professional and technical occupations. A survey in one Southwestern city revealed that Latinos speaking only Spanish earn 18% less than those who are bilingual. Thus, it would appear that the audience attracted by XXX would have little attraction for advertisers. How the station sells this audience to advertisers is the focus of this section.

Sales Organization. The XXX sales department, which has the responsibility for selling the audience, was comprised of a sales manager and five sales positions. The station was also represented nationally by a national advertising representative. The sales manager concentrated on servicing national accounts and divided responsibilities for different types of accounts with the remainder of the staff. One concentrated on selling local chain operations and agencies. Another focused on retail accounts with businesses catering primarily to Chicanos, such as furniture stores. The three other positions were filled by newcomers who sought accounts from retail outlets wherever they could find them.

Advertising Policies. Most of the advertising on XXX is spot advertising, which means the advertiser pays for a one-minute or thirty-second commercial announcement that is broadcast at different times. Advertising rates are determined by the nature of the audience when they are aired and the number of spots the advertiser buys over the year. Rates ranged from $50 for a single one-minute spot to $25 per one-minute spot for an advertiser buying 1,000 or more a year.

Rates include translation of copy to Spanish and production of spots at the station if desired. Advertising agencies that produce their own spots and bill advertisers are granted a 15% commission (discount) by the station. All spots aired on the station were pre-recorded on cartridges and played by disc jockeys according to a schedule devised by the XXX traffic department.

Selling XXX and Its Audience. XXX's sales department faces a threefold task in selling itself and its audience to advertisers. First, advertisers must be convinced that Chicanos comprise a desirable consuming public. Second, they must be convinced that XXX is the most effective way of penetrating and persuading that market. And, third, they must be persuaded that XXX advertising is cost effective; that they will extract more money from the audience than they will invest in advertising on the station.

In addressing the first concern XXX's sales department uses a variety of tools to establish the commercial viability of the Chicano audience. In order to dispel the image of low-income consumers the XXX sales materials stress the size of the Chicano audience in the market and talk in terms of collective "annual buying power." In so doing the station relies heavily on census data and studies by local and regional planning agencies.

The station also uses news clippings which cite the steady growth of the Latino community in the area and compares the size of the local Chicano community with other large markets in the nation. They also point to characteristics of Chicanos that make them potentially desirable to advertisers. One salesman explained how family sizes are used to sell the audience:

> Mexican American people, being what they are, are usually a a larger family. They do their shopping together and they buy more products because they are a larger family. So it only makes sense that if they're a larger family they're going to buy more and it's going to increase the sales of those advertisers and brokers.

Having established the viability of the Chicano audience as a market, the station then turns to establishing XXX as the most effective way of reaching and persuading that audience. "SELL THEM WITH THE MOST EFFECTIVE MEDIA IN THE MARKET, RADIO XXX," states one promotional flyer. Other materials compare audience sizes with other Spanish-language media as reported by commercial media rating services. These materials stress the drawing power of XXX for persons in the 18–49 age category desired by most advertisers. One sheet for grocery chains claims XXX listeners have large families and "that means more mouths to feed and more that must be spent on food." Comparisons with other Spanish-language radio stations invariably show XXX on top of the station's promotional materials.

The ratings have become increasingly important to the XXX sales arsenal, not only because of the station's top ranking but because advertising agencies make decisions based on them. The vice president and general manager asserted "the ratings have a big power over our business" and noted that even small businesses are deciding which media to buy based on them:

> It's only in the last, not even two years, that there has been an acceptance on the part of the less sophisticated retail advertiser who, when we give him the figures, would always say, "Estas cifras no me importan." These figures now become important to him because he begins to realize that they are a measurement... that you have to have figures in order to gain some kind of knowledge of what you're getting for your money."

Having argued for the commercial viability of the Chicano audience and the audience size of XXX, the station's sales force must then convince potential advertisers that advertising on XXX persuades Latinos to spend money. In order to do this the station subscribes to an advertising service which monitors movement of products in markets. The service compares movement of goods in Anglo and Chicano neighborhoods and this comparison can be a powerful tool in closing a sale with a new or skeptical XXX advertiser. One salesman outlined how he used the service's computerized reports to make a sale:

> To initiate a sale I'll call up a regional manager or sales district product manager and try to set up an appointment; telling him what I just got on the computer printout. And salesmen, being the way they are, they're always interested in their figures. So it's pretty easy to open up the door in getting in to see these managers. Then after I see them I start discussing the Spanish people and the movement of their product.

Armed with the impartiality of the computer printouts and examples of how other products have moved after advertising on XXX, the salesman then tries to have the advertiser make a test purchase of XXX advertising and wait for the results of the next computer printout. If advertising is purchased then the next printouts should show increased sales of the product in the Chicano neighborhood markets.

Analysis of Advertising. In order to gain an understanding of who was advertising on XXX an analysis of advertisers listed on program logs for a composite week covering one year was performed. Advertisers were coded by the type of product, store or service they represented (see Table 3). The results showed that the greatest percentage of advertising was generated by individual retail outlets (15%) and food and beverages (15%). Next came chain retail outlets (11%) and public events (11%). These top four categories comprised 52% of the station's advertisers. The combination of individual and chain retail outlets alone accounted for 26%. Thus, the station was primarily dependent on stores, products, and public events for most of its advertising, with stores accounting for more than a quarter of the advertisers.

Since XXX sales personnel indicated that the station was drawing increasing income from national and regional advertisers and from advertising agencies, the station accounting office was asked to provide a five-year comparison of billings. The data revealed that agency-placed advertising had increased from 69% to 81% of XXX's advertising during the previous five years. However, a second analysis performed by the staff indicated that most of the increase had come through increased sales to locally-based advertising agencies, not through sales to national advertisers. In the same five years national advertising agency billings dropped from 40% of the station's agency billings to 30%. Since adver-

75

TABLE 3: Frequency Distribution of XXX Advertisers by Type of Advertiser

Type of Advertiser	Number	Percent
Individual Retail Outlets (Furniture stores, automobile dealers, etc.	23	15
Food and Beverages (Beer, wine, soft drinks, food products)	23	15
Chain or Group Retail Outlets (Automobile dealer associations, grocer chains, department stores)	16	11
Public Events (Dances, sporting events, shows, amusement parks)	17	11
Schools (Driving and trade schools)	9	6
Theaters, Restaurants, and Night Clubs	9	6
Services (Immigration counseling, abortion clinics)	7	5
Drugs and Medicinals	7	5
Personal Care Products	7	5
Household Products	6	4
Other Media (Newspapers, records)	5	3
Financial Institutions (Finance companies)	3	2
Automotive Services	4	3
Public Utilities	2	1
Airlines	2	1
Food Take Out Chains	2	1
Appliances	1	1
Political Candidates	1	1
Unknown	6	4
Total	150	100

Source: Annual Composite Week (Advertisers coded for presence only, no duplications for multiple insertions. Cooperative advertisements coded by retail outlet.)

tising revenues were up in all categories the decline in national billing percentages was a relative one, not one of actual dollars. Thus, the analysis of billings indicates station XXX is becoming more dependent on advertising placed by agencies, not local businesses who have the commercials taped at the station, and that the largest growth in agency billings has been at the local level.

Revenue and Profit. The station provided general figures regarding revenue and profit and other figures were gained from materials filed with the FCC. The station's financial statement with its license renewal early in the 1970s revealed total assets and liabilities of slightly over $1 million. In interviews billings were also reported to be "close to a million dollars." The vice-president and general manager estimated that operating costs "absorbed half the revenue before you even start to work." He was quick to add that the remainder was not all profit, since it was used to pay for staff, outside production work, sales commissions, and paying off the debt used to buy the station. He did not report how much was profit. But an annual balance sheet filed by the station in the early 1970s listed retained earnings of just over $1 million. Retained earnings are stockholder's equity that has arisen out of the corporation's operation and includes both income generated through normal operation and one-shot earnings, such as sale of assets.

Entertainment Programming

XXX's entertainment programming is the major bait used to attract listeners to the station, a point underscored by the fact that the station devotes 87% of its broadcast time to entertainment. The sound offered on the entertainment programming is a heavily-formatted mixture of music, taped announcements, jingles, and contests. The format minimizes the role of the disc jockey, who is supposed to play a recorded message to even say his name, and maximizes the music and consistency of jingles and advertising by recording them in advance.

The current format was adopted when the owner found that the personality format that then dominated the station allowed for too much variation in music and attracted an older audience. He decided to program a sound that would attract the younger listeners advertisers wanted to reach. So the station switched to a Top 40 format, which meant the management selected the music, disc jockeys were instructed to talk less, and messages were pre-recorded. In the process most of the old XXX disc jockeys, many of them former brokers, left the station.

The evolution of the Top 40 format was a strictly economic decision designed to attract a younger audience and discourage listening by older, often longtime listeners. The switch was made in order to attract an audience that would be more saleable to advertising agencies. The vice president and general manager described how the programming change affected the composition of the audience:

> This was a decision (to change the music) we made because you cannot obviously discourage anyone or prohibit anyone from listening to your radio station. . . . But you can, and we have proven it with the studies made by the regular survey companies, change the composition of your audience from a plus 50 with a very few young 18 and over to an audience that is now almost 90% composed of 18 to 49. Now we could not do this any other way except by playing the music that people 49 or 50 plus would not be comfortable with.

Staff Organization. The entertainment programming of the station is under the direction of the program director and his staff. During the mid-1970s the station employed nine full time announcers who had primary responsibilities as disc jockeys, but also broadcast some news and recorded advertisements. Most of the disc jockeys were in their late 20s and early 30s and, as noted earlier, came to XXX after working in broadcasting in Latin America.

The music played on XXX was selected from records brought to the station by record promoters, agents for musical groups and singers, and regional record distributors. Because of the potential of payola influencing the selection of records to be aired, the station had a policy limiting contact between promoters and disc jockeys. The records were left with the station receptionist and were auditioned each week by the program director and disc jockeys individually. The group would meet once a week to discuss the records that had been left and make recommendations on which should be aired. Final decisions were made by the program director with the approval of the vice president and general manager.

Playlists. XXX has a weekly playlist listing the records it will play each week. The list is divided into three sections. The main list, called the Top 40 éxitos, lists 40 songs that the station considers to be current hits. The second list, called the pronósticos, is a list of 10 new songs selected from records left at the station. A third list of songs, called recuerdos, lists 10 songs that had been popular within the past few years. All songs played on XXX for a given week must be listed on the playlists and disc jockeys are required to play each of the 60 songs before one can be repeated. They can, however, decide the order in which the songs will be played on their segments.

Once a song is selected for the pronósticos list it automatically moves to the éxitos list the following week. In order to determine which songs are to be kept on the éxitos list from week to week the programming staff calls four record stores each week and reads the list of records on the éxitos list. The record stores, which are rotated weekly, indicate whether sales for each record are up or down for that week. Records selling well are kept on the list for another week (for a maximum of six weeks) and those that are not are deleted.

In order to insure that different types of music are played the station divides the records into three types of Latino music: (1) *música moderna* or modern music; (2) *tropicales* or tropical music; and (3) *rancheras/norteñas* or music from the northern frontier of México. The station plays only new releases in these three categories and will play traditional songs only if they have been released in modernized versions.

The selection of music is heavily weighted toward the *música mo-*

derna category. An analysis of the playlists for a six month period revealed that 62% of the music was *música moderna,* 20% was *rancheras* and 18% *tropicales.* According to the program director this is the balance the station wants to maintain to attract the younger audience its advertisers desire.

The playlists and the consistency of music form the identifiable sound which the station hopes to present to its listeners. It is a sound that the audience will hear no matter what time of the day or night it turns to the station. But the consistency of the music is only one element of the XXX "sound." The manner in which the music is presented is another important part.

Format. XXX presents its music in a tightly-formatted, almost mechanical, manner that calls for a maximum of pre-recorded jingles, advertisements, and promotional tapes and a minimum of talk by the disc jockey. The announcers' responsibilities include selecting and cueing records or tapes from the playlists, punching up tape cartridges of commercials and jingles, keeping the log, answering the telephone, and airing pre-recorded contests. The least of their responsibilities is talking over the air.

The closely packaged XXX format calls for the disc jockey to follow a predetermined pattern through his airtime. The pattern, starting with the introduction of a record, calls for the announcer to play the first bars of the song and then voice over the name of the song and performer. While the record is playing the disc jockeys replace the song previously played with a new one, note the song being played on the playlist, check the log for scheduled commercials or public service announcements, locate and punch up the pre-taped cartridges for advertisements and public service announcements, cue the next song, and, as the last strains of the song on the turntable are playing, again announce the name of the song and group. When the song is finished the disc jockey quickly gives the time of day and proceeds to a fast series of pre-recorded advertisements, jingles or public service announcements. Somewhere in between he will usually give the temperature and restate the time. If he wants to remind the audience of his name he is supposed to punch up a pre-recorded identification tape. Then he proceeds with the next song.

Analysis of Music Sources. A common observation of those familiar with Spanish-language radio in the Southwest is that the stations are heavily dependent on music from Latin America and do not give sufficient air play to local musicians or to music recorded by Latinos in the United States. In a preliminary interview XXX's program director estimated that 75% of the station's music came from Latin America. In order to gain a more precise understanding of the extent of XXX's dependence on imported records an analysis of a complete year's pronósticos lists were analyzed. The playlists represent all the records introduced on XXX for that year.

The survey was performed by recording the names of all the record labels aired. The program director was then asked to identify the country of origin for the labels. The labels were then coded into four categories: (1) United States, (2) foreign country, (3) multinational corporation, and (4) unknown. It should be noted that the record label does not necessarily indicate the nationality of the artists, only the origin of the record. Similarly, multinational corporations will release records under the same label in different countries.

The analysis revealed that of the 118 separate labels represented on the 520 songs introduced that year (see Table 4) the largest percentage (48%) was on foreign labels. This was followed by United States labels (33%), multinational corporations (12%), and labels of unknown origin (6%). Because of the concern about depending on foreign sources for programming, the station tabulates the number of local groups whose records were being played each week. This count ranged between four and eight records each week and averaged about five, 10% of the records on the weekly playlist for that period.

Airplay Impact. The concern about airplay for local groups partially illustrates the potential power of XXX over the success of local musicians. That potential also affects the success of record promotions, dances, and theatrical performances. One administrator for the United States subsidiary of a large Latin American record company said the record companies placed heavy emphasis on gaining playing time for their records on Spanish-language radio stations. A dance promoter

TABLE 4:   Frequency Distribution of Records Played on XXX by Record Label
Country of Origin

Country of Origin	Number	Percent
United States Label	174	33
Foreign Country Label	250	48
Multinational Corporation Label	63	12
Unknown Origin Label	33	6
Total	520	99

Source: XXX Pronósticos Playlists and XXX Program Director.

said that Latin American groups were often selected for United States tours based partially on whether or not their records were being played on Spanish-language stations.

When asked about the importance of XXX airplay on the sale of records the program director replied:

> Unfortunately, the station has become so powerful, it has so much impact in our community, that a record we don't play won't sell.

Because of this power XXX management limits contact between disc jockeys and record promoters, requires disc jockeys to report when they have taken outside jobs as masters of ceremonies and performers, and prohibits on-the-air interviews with artists performing in town. The station also will not put songs on its prognósticos list by groups scheduled to appear locally, although groups already on the éxitos list may continue to have their records played.

News programming

News comprises about 10% of XXX's broadcast time and, like most Top 40 stations, is delivered in short newscasts aired at regular intervals throughout the broadcast day. The news on XXX is delivered in a fast-paced, almost breathless, manner that maximizes the number of items covered but rarely probes any in depth. Newscasts are scheduled at half-hour intervals, with news headlines preceding them five minutes before.

The vice president and general manager explained how the news format blended with the station's Top 40 entertainment sound:

> We have found with the news that if we went beyond a three and a half minute newscast we would begin to lose the audience. Because what we found was that most people would like to have their news delivered in a rapid, clear style and that if you could pack 14, maybe 15, items with two voices you could manage to do that in three or three and a half minutes. The moment you start going beyond that the itchy finger would turn the dial and you start to lose the audience.

Organization. The news operation is supervised by the news director who reports to the program director. The news director supervised the two other announcers who worked primarily with news and the four announcers who worked news in addition to other responsibilities. He described XXX's news format as "trying to say the greatest number of things possible in the least space." Most of the news is taken from wire

81

services, with the station subscribing both to the national and Spanish-language Latin American wires of one of the major wire services. The newscasters operate in the traditional "rip and read" manner characterizing many broadcast news operations, with the exception that English-language copy is translated and most Spanish-language copy is tightened to conform with XXX's rapid delivery format. News content is changed with every newscast, which means the newscasters are kept busy selecting and writing copy between casts.

Analysis of News Content. Both the program director and news director stressed in interviews that the station emphasized reporting local news. In its license renewal the station management indicated about half of the station's news time "has been and will continue to be devoted to local and regional news." In order to assess the station's performance against these promises a content analysis of items broadcast on the news for a composite week was performed. The analysis covered five randomly distributed newscasts per day for a period of seven days. The newscasts were recorded and the contents coded according to nominal categories.

The first item coded was origin of the story. Since announcers always give the story's dateline the datelines were coded into one of four categories: (1) local, (2) state exclusive of local counties, (3) national exclusive of state, and (4) international. Of the 175 news items coded the greatest percentage (34%) came from outside the United States, primarily Latin America (see Table 5A). Next came state stories (27%) and national stories (23%). Local stories were last at 16%.

The second item coded was whether or not the story was specifically related to the Chicano community. An item was considered Chicano related if the story was presented in a way stressing its impact on Chicanos, if it featured a Chicano spokesperson, if it emanated from a

TABLE 5A: Frequency Distribution of XXX News Items by Place of Origin

Origin	Number	Percent
Local	28	16
State	48	27
National	40	23
Latin America	31	18
International	28	16
Total	175	100

Source: Composite Week.

Category	Number	Percent
Chicano Related	8	5
Not Chicano Related	167	95
Total	175	100

Source: Composite Week.

Chicano group, or if it offered opportunities of special interest to Latinos. Items from Latin America were not coded as Chicano related unless reference was made to Latinos in the United States. Of the 175 items coded nearly all (95%) were non-Chicano related (see Table 5B). Only eight of the items broadcast contained references specifically related to the listening audience.

Despite the professed commitment of XXX management to airing local items, the distribution of news items should not be surprising. In depending so heavily on wire services for news copy the station links itself to a news source that is more national and international than local. Since the station employed a field reporter on a limited basis and did not subscribe to a local news service, there would be a reduced opportunity for local items to reach the attention of the newscasters.

Public Service Programming

XXX's license renewal form states the station devotes nearly three percent of its broadcast time to public affairs programming. The programming, which is required of all stations by the FCC, is supposed to be used to disseminate information and discussion of issues important to the audience. Such programming is particularly important to the audiences of Spanish-language radio, who have less access to other media than those speaking English.

XXX offers a wide variety of public affairs programs, most tailored to fit within the station's Top 40 program format. This means most of the station's commitment is fulfilled by broadcasting short announcements scattered throughout the broadcast day, rather than devoting large blocks of time to discussion or interview programs. Only one program featured a long block of time for public affairs and was aired live for an hour each week.

The vice president and general manager explained that public service programs were designed to be consistent with the "faithful kind of sound" listeners expect when they turn to XXX. In order to do this the station packages public service messages like commercials in 30 and 60 second spot announcements. He explained:

> For example, for two and a half years we carried, at the suggestion of the public health authorities, a one-minute commercial which said "this is how you can improve your health" or "this is how you can rearrange your life," instead of a 15-minute talk. We decided that we had to sell on the basis of commercial time."

This method allows the station to deliver public service announcements with a minimal disruption of the Top 40 format and, according to the management, deliver a message "as though it was a series of commercials selling food or service."

Organization. XXX's public service programs include health, consumer, and job information provided by different public agencies. These programs, which are generated by governmental sources outside of the station, account for about four hours a week. The programming the station produces itself include a weekly call in program, a community bulletin board of local events aired five times daily, and public service announcements. The station also does occasional remote broadcasts from community events of a public service nature.

Analysis of La Tribuna Pública. La Tribuna Pública is a weekly hourlong program featuring different guests each week. The guests are interviewed by members of the XXX staff and also answer questions phoned in by listeners. The program is taped and rebroadcast again later in the the week. The show is aired both times in the evening hours, a time calculated to do least damage to the ratings according to the program director. It was when reaction to the show proved favorable that the station decided to rebroadcast the tape a second evening. When asked if XXX planned to go beyond this two hour commitment the program director said he didn't want to "saturate" the station with such programming.

The purpose of *La Tribuna Pública* is to provide public officials and organizations an opportunity to speak and answer questions on topics of interest to the Chicano community. However, the coordinator of the program noted that some public agencies were reluctant to send representatives to the Spanish-language station and that others could not find employees who were conversant in Spanish.

An analysis of *La Tribuna Pública* guests was performed to determine what type of organizations used the program most often. The results indicated that the time used about equally by government agencies and government funded projects (35%) and Latino community

84

TABLE 6: Frequency Distribution of *La Tribuna Pública* Guests by Type of Organization Represented

Type of Organization or Government	Number	Percent
Government Agency or Government Funded Project	18	34
Latino Organization	18	35
Other	5	10
No Show	11	21
Total	52	101

Source: *La Tribuna Pública* calendar and coordinator.

organizations (35%) (see Table 6). Following were weeks in which no program was aired (21%) and persons not fitting in the two main categories (10%), such as a self-proclaimed mental telepathy expert.

The program coordinator described the program as an opportunity to give Latino organizations much need exposure to their community and to raise issues of importance to the Chicano community to public officials and politicians "who often do not give the deserved attention" to their Spanish-speaking constituents. However, the management in its license application described the program as an attempt to give the Chicano community "a dose of preventive medicine" in seeking redress for long-standing grievances. For instance, the station proposed to treat "the major problems of police-community relations and the language barrier" in the following way:

We propose to do this in an affirmative way, for example, by emphasizing the advantage that a bilingual person has in seeking employment in this area. The needs of the police and sheriff's departments for applicants with bilingual ability will also be publicized. . . .

Thus, the station indicated it did not intend to probe or investigate the causes of problems. Instead, it planned to focus on positive ways in which its Spanish-speaking listeners could cope with them.

Analysis of Community Notices. Another way in which XXX provides public notices of interest to its audience is through the bulletin board of community events recorded and broadcast at different times during the day. The notices are designed to allow local organizations an opportunity to publicize their upcoming public events and run about three minutes. Since the recorded announcements are aired at different times of the day and night an analysis was performed to determine which times were used most often for the broadcast.

85

TABLE 7: Frequency Distribution of Community Notices Airtimes

Airtime	Number	Percent
7 to Midnight	5	18
Midnight–6 a.m.	13	46
6 to 10	2	7
10 to 3 p.m.	6	21
3 to 7	2	7
Total	28	99

Source: Composite Week.

The results, which were based on a composite week for an entire year, indicated the community notices were aired most often between midnight and 6 a.m. (46%) (see Table 7). Next followed the mid-morning/early afternoon time slot (21%) and the 7 p.m. to midnight time period (18%). The morning and early evening drive time segments accounted for only 2% of the programs apiece. Thus, 64% of the time the notices were aired they were broadcast between 7 p.m. and 6 a.m., when XXX's audience is lowest. The time periods selected for classification were based on the dayparts used by the commercial rating services.

Analysis of Public Service Announcements. Public service announcements (PSAs) are another vehicle community organizations could use to reach the XXX audience. On XXX PSAs are pre-recorded as one minute or 30-second spot announcements, much like commercials, for non-profit, governmental, public service or community groups. XXX airs about 60 PSAs a daily selected on a monthly basis from the estimated 600 proposed PSAs it receives in the mail each month. The program director selects the PSAs to be aired each month and they are then translated and recorded on taped cartridges. Some arrive at the station with Spanish copy or recorded in Spanish, but most arrive only with English-language scripts. The program director says he picks those PSAs "which I consider are a help to our community."

Once selected for airing the PSAs are then turned over to XXX's traffic director for scheduling throughout the broadcast day on the station's log. The traffic director said PSAs are generally scheduled for the evening and early morning hours because "there are more commercials during the day." Thus, the PSAs are scheduled around commercials and generally are placed at the less desirable commercial times.

In order to understand which types of organizations were heard most often on XXX's PSAs, an analysis of the sources for XXX PSAs was performed. The results showed that the majority of XXX's PSAs (53%) came from government agencies or government funded projects (see Table 8A). Next came private agencies or special interest associations, such as the American Cancer Society (38%), voluntary associations, such as the Junior Chamber of Commerce (5%) and others (4%). Thus, most of XXX's PSAs were allocated to governmentally related organizations, not to local groups. Only two organizations from within the Latino community had PSAs aired on the Spanish-language station that year.

The preponderance of governmental and special interest PSAs may be attributable to XXX's policy of selecting PSAs only once a month. Since all PSAs must be received in the month prior to broadcast and must be usable for the entire following month, the policy favors organizations which can anticipate their PSA needs in advance and can provide copy that is not time related. Thus, most of the XXX PSAs are general or broad-based messages on such topics as safe driving.

A second analysis was performed on the 145 PSAs for that year on which copy was available. This analysis included 75% of the PSAs broadcast that year, but did not include those which had been pre-recorded and sent to the station. The PSA scripts were coded as to whether or not they contained information relating to the special needs, or interests of the Spanish-speaking audience. These included such items as services for the Spanish speaking, alien registration, or materials of special interest to Latinos. The results indicated that of the 145 PSAs analyzed only 26% had information specifically related to the Spanish-speaking audience (see Table 8B). The remaining were of general public interest, such as highway safety. Some had been trans-

TABLE 8A: Frequency Distribution of Public Service Announcements by Type of Sponsor

Category	Number	Percent
Government Agency or Government-funded Project	102	53
Private Agencies, Charities and Special Interest Associations	74	38
Voluntary Associations	9	5
Other	8	4
Total	193	100

Source: XXX Public Service Announcement logs and XXX traffic director.

TABLE 8B: Frequency Distribution of Public Service Announcements Not Pre-Recorded by the Sponsor by Relationship to Chicano Audience

Category	Number	Percent
Specifically Related to Chicano Audience	38	26
Not Specifically Related to Chicano Audience	107	74
Total	145	100

Source: Copy for XXX Public Service Announcements.

lated from English-language PSAs offering booklets on topic of interest. The XXX staff had translated the PSAs into Spanish even though their was no indication on the original copy that Spanish-language booklets were available.

A final analysis was performed to determine the times as which XXX broadcasts its PSAs, similar to the analysis performed on the community notices. Again the broadcast day was divided according to the divisions used by the rating services and again the analysis revealed that of the 413 PSAs aired during the composite week the greatest number were heard between 7 p.m. and 6 a.m. (82%) when the audience was lowest (see Table 9). Thus, less than 20% of the PSAs aired on the station were broadcast during times when listenership was high.

Audience Characteristics

Although they may not realize it, the listeners are potentially the ultimate source of power over XXX and any other commercial radio station. This is because the economic viability of the station is ultimately dependent on the size and composition of its listening audience. The bottom line on whether or not advertisers will invest money in a station is based primarily on whether or not anyone is listening to the

TABLE 9: Frequency Distribution of Public Service Announcement Airtimes

Airtime	Number	Percent
7 p.m. to Midnight	168	41
Midnight to 6 a.m.	171	41
6 a.m. to 10 a.m.	22	5
10 a.m. to 3 p.m.	11	3
3 p.m. to 7 p.m.	41	10
Total	413	100

Source: Composite Week.

station and what the listeners' characteristics are. It is this information that the station gathers on its audience that is used to sell advertising time to potential advertisers. Without a saleable audience no commercial radio station can profitably survive. This section addresses the question: Who is the XXX audience?

Audience Rating Services. Measuring the size and composition of the XXX audience are two commercial audience rating services, which produce bi-monthly reports on all radio stations in the market. The commercial rating services have been under long criticism from Black and Spanish-language radio stations for their alleged inability to adequately measure minority communities. While the XXX vice president and general manager conceded that Spanish-language stations often got the "short end of the stick" in the ratings because of inadequate representation of Latinos in the sample, the station continues to use them because it usually ranked above the other Spanish-language stations.

The ratings by both services indicate that the XXX management has been successful in attracting the listeners in the 18–49 age category that advertising agencies desire. Men between 18 and 49 comprised about 80% of XXX's male listeners and women between 18 and 49 comprised about 90% of the female audience for all time periods. In terms of total audience size, the estimates ranged between 30,000 and 45,000 for daytime periods. This compared quite favorably when measured against other radio stations, Spanish or English, in the market. XXX usually ranked among the top five stations in the market for female listeners during the daytime and in one survey was reported as having the largest 18 to 49 female daytime audience of any station in the area.

An analysis of listeners by demographic characteristics performed by a commercial rating service revealed that XXX listeners are highly concentrated in lower socio-economic groups. The survey showed that 60% of the station's male listeners and 88% of the female listeners over 18 years old lived in households with annual incomes under $10,000. Thirty-two percent of the men and 24% of the women had annual household incomes under $5,000. An analysis by the same service of employment revealed XXX listeners in both blue and white collar occupations, but few working as professionals, managers or sales. These figures indicate XXX's listeners generally live in lower-income households and have jobs below the professional, manager or sales classifications.

XXX Audience by Place of Residence. Although the commercial rating services indicate age, sex, and limited demographic information on a radio station's audience, they do not provide information on where listeners live. This information can be important because it can be used as an indicator of other socioeconomic characteristics of the audience.

In order to determine the residential characteristics of the XXX audience an analysis of the zip codes of XXX audience participation contest winners for periods over a year was performed. Although the contest winners do not represent the entire XXX audience, they would indicate which areas have the highest participation in the contest and, presumably, highest identification with the station. The station has two audience participation contests. Both contests are broadcast each hour and required little expertise to win.

The analysis was performed by recording the zip codes for the 1811 winners of the contests for the periods surveyed, listing the number of winners for each zip code, and then recording socioeconomic information for each zip code area from analyses of census data by city, county and regional planning agencies. This information included the number of Latinos living in the area, the percentage of the population of that area that Latinos comprise, and the median family income for Latinos in that area. All of this information was recorded on cards with the number of XXX contest winners for that area. The final compilation consisted of 124 cards representing the districts capable of receiving the station's daytime signal. The cards were then divided into equal quarters by income and the quarters compared to determine the percentage of Latino residents with the percentage of XXX winners in each quarter. The purpose of the analysis was to determine if XXX contest winners were evenly distributed across the Latino population by income or were concentrated in certain economic areas.

TABLE 10A: Comparison of XXX Audience Participation Contest Winners as Grouped Latino Median Family Income of Place of Residence

	First Quarter	Second Quarter	Second Quarter	Fourth Quarter
Income Range	$4,354– $8,476	$8,576– $9,744	$ 9,932– $11,402	$11,454– $35,700
Median Income	$7,986	$8,992	$10,570	$13,362
Percent of Total Latinos	48%	22%	22%	8%
Percent of XXX Winners	73%	14%	10%	3%

Sources: XXX Audience Participation Contest Winners, 1970 Fourth Count Census Tapes.

The results indicated that XXX's contest winners were heavily concentrated in the lower Latino income areas (see Table 10A). The first, or lowest income quartile accounted for 48% of the Latino population, but 73% of the contest winners. The second, next lowest income, quartile accounted for 22% of the Latino population and 14% of the winners. The third quartile also accounted for 22% of the Latino populatoni, but 10% of the winners. The fourth, highest income, quartile accounted for 8% of the Latino population and only 3% of the contest winners. Thus, the analysis revealed an overrepresentation of XXX contest winners among Latinos living in low income areas and an underrepresentation among Latinos living in moderate and upper income areas. Chi Square analysis for independence of cells revealed these differences in distribution significant to the .001 level (see Table 10B).

XXX Listeners in a Low Income Neighborhood. In order to gain an understanding of the characteristics of XXX listeners in a low income area such as those that comprised the majority of its contest winners an, analysis of an additional data set was performed. These data had been gathered in a media use survey of residents of low income Chicano neighborhood. Among other questions, respondents were asked to name their favorite radio station. About 25% named XXX, 25% named other Spanish-language radio stations, 36% named English-language radio stations, and 12% indicated no preference. The analysis performed compared XXX listeners with those preferring an English-language station to determine if there were differences in socioeconomic characteristics of English- and Spanish-language radio listeners in other categories explored by that survey.

The analysis showed statistically significant differences between XXX listeners and English-language listeners in both demographic and media use characteristics (see Table 11). Those preferring the Spanish-language station tended to be older than those preferring English-

TABLE 10B: Crosstabulation of XXX Audience Participation Contest Winners by Latino Median Family Income of Place of Residence

Income Quartile	Percent of Latino Residents	Percent of XXX Winners
Quartile I	48	73
Quartile II	23	15
Quartile III	22	10
Quartile IV	8	3

Source: XXX Contest Winners   S=.001

Summary Crosstabulation of Differences Between XXX and English-language Radio Listeners in a Low Income Area

Crosstabulation Variables	Chi Square Level of Significance
Age of Respondents	S=.001
Years of Education	S=.01
Length of Residence	S=.01
Employment	S=.01
Ethnic Label	S=.001
Language Preference	S=.001
Newspaper Preference	S=.10
Magazine Preference	S=.001
Television Station Preference	S=.01

Source: Low Income Neighborhood Survey.

language stations. They also tended to be less educated, more recent arrivals to the area, and more highly concentrated in semiskilled or unskilled occupations. XXX listeners also tended to be retired, housewives or unemployed when compared with English-language radio listeners and showed a significant preference for the self identification term of Mexicano. English-language listeners showed a preference for a wider variety of ethnic identification terms, such as Mexican American or Chicano, or indicated no preference. The analysis also showed a higher preference for other Spanish-language print and electronic media by XXX listeners than by their neighbors preferring English-language radio.

Summary of the XXX Audience Chracteristics. The different sources of information in this section have provided a data base on which some generalizations about XXX's audience can be made. From the information generated by the commercial rating services it is possible to conclude that the station has been successful in attracting the 18–49 age group desired by its advertisers and that the station's audience is quite large when compared with other Spanish and English-language radio stations. The rating services also draw a demographic profile of XXX listeners as being in lower income households and working at nonprofessional jobs.

The analysis of winners of XXX audience participation contests indicates that this group of active XXX listeners is highly concentrated in low income Latino neighborhoods, as compared with middle or upper income Latino areas. The survey of residents of a low income Chicano neighborhood indicates that XXX listeners tend to be older, less educated, more recent arrivals, and less likely to be bilingual than those preferring English-language radio. They were also more likely to prefer other Spanish-language media than those using English-language radio.

Audience Feedback

Like any media organization XXX is dependent on a certain amount of feedback from its audience to survive and grow. The amount of feedback a station receives from its audience and the way it is used is determined by the needs of the station. In this section three types of audience feedback are analyzed, they are: (1) ascertainment of community needs as required by the FCC, (2) formal feedback mechanisms initiated by the station and regularly used by it, and (3) informal feedback mechanisms initiated by the audience and irregularly used by the station.

Ascertainment of Community Needs. The FCC requires broadcasters to ascertain the needs of the communities they serve when they apply for renewal of their broadcast license every three years. The ascertainment is divided into two sections. One section involves community leaders and usually takes the form of a personal interview. The second section is a survey of the general public, which often is done over the telephone.

In its license renewal XXX's management interviewed 28 community leaders from "a broad range of agencies and organizations." These included law enforcement, administrative officials, public service agencies, and Chicano community groups. Of the 28 persons interviewed (13) (46%) were affiliated either which Latino communities or agencies working in the Latino community and an additional five (18%) were Spanish-surnamed employees of non-Latino agencies or organizations. Thus, 64% of the community leaders ascertained by XXX had a direct involvement with the Spanish-speaking community that comprises the station's audience.

The interviews of the general public were less reflective of the station's Latino audience. Since the station is licensed to a city in a large metropolitan area, not to the Chicano community, a random telephone survey of the entire community was performed by the station for its public ascertainment. The station did not reveal in its license renewal application how interviewees were chosen (other than to say a random selection was used) or how many calls were made.

The purpose of the ascertainment is to assist the station in identifying community issues which it can address in its programming. The survey identified few international or national problems, other than taxes, but a number of local problems were mentioned. The station ranked these problems in order of frequency and depth as: police-community relations, language barriers, militancy, need for recreational facilities, problems of the elderly (especially transportation), employment, need for veterans information, housing (crowding inadequate city services), absence of "good news," and effectiveness of the judicial system.

Half of the problems mentioned (police-community relations, recreational facilties, veterans information, housing and judicial system) are directly related to areas of governmental responsibility. Three others (language barriers, militancy, and absence of good news) are problems which are peculiar to, or have special meaning for, the Chicano community. The other two (problems of the elderly and employment) are societal problems with additional implications for the Chicano community. Thus, most of the problems listed are either related to government responsibilities or special problems encountered by Latinos in the United States.

Although XXX's license renewal application pledged to "treat the above-described problems and others which continuously come to its attention in the day-to-day operation of the station," the only programs specifically designed to address the expressed problems were in the areas of public service programming. Since public service programs make up only a small percentage of the station's broadcast hours and are often aired at times when audiences are minimal, the effect of the ascertainment on programming is not great. The ascertainment is also limited in that it is undertaken only once every three years and, in terms of the general public survey, is not specifically directed at the Latino community that comprises the station's audience.

Formal Feedback Mechanisms. The XXX managment uses at least three forms of formal audience feedback loops to generate information which the station feels is important. These are: (1) commercial rating services, (2) the survey of grocery purchases, and (3) the weekly phone calls to record stores. The operation of each of these feedback mechanisms was discussed earlier in the chapter at the points where they affected the station's operation. In this section the utility of these audience feedback tools will be analyzed in terms of the type of information they provide to the station and the manner in which they define feedback from the audience.

The commercial rating services are basically indicators of who is listening to the station. The station uses this information to prove to advertisers that it has an audience and to describe the characteristics of

94

the audience. This allows the advertiser to direct messages at times when the audience is largest or has desired demographic characteristics. The commercial ratings are important because they are conducted by an independent organization, carry the image of impartiality, and allow XXX to make comparisons between itself and other stations. Thus, they are an important tool in the arsenal used to attract advertisers.

In terms of audience feedback the rating services channel only a certain type of information to the station. It is information based on consumption of the station's programming. The ratings tell only how many people are listening at different times of the day and what their characteristics are. It does not tell how satisfied they are with the programming, how well they are listening, or what they like or don't like about the station. Thus, it channels only the feedback which is useful to the economic interests of the station and its advertisers.

The grocery shipment reports are a second form of feedback. These reports measure the movement of items in grocery stores in Latino and non-Latino neighborhoods. The station's advertising department uses these reports as indicators of the effectiveness of advertising on XXX and they also carry the image of impartial verification of the station's impact. Although the reports are probably not essential to the operation of the station, they do provide an independent means for an advertiser to check the effect of XXX advertising.

Like the rating services, the grocery reports are also a measure of audience consumption; in this case the consumption of products advertised on the station. The feedback mechanism is limited in that it measures only consumption at certain markets. This excludes purchases made elsewhere. It is also difficult to isolate the specific impact of XXX advertising relative to other factors which might affect sales.

The third audience feedback loop used regularly by the station is the weekly phone calls to record stores to determine which songs on the playlists are selling well. This mechanism is important to determining which songs will be played on the station and, as such, is an important factor in deciding the entertainment programming the audience will hear. Like the others it also carries the image of being an impartial way for the audience to indicate it desires to the station through a third party.

Like the other methods, the telephone calls to record stores is also a measure of consumption; in this case the purchase of records played on the station. It is also limited in the type of information it carries. First, the reliability of the information is probably variable. A record store operator may have an accurate estimate of what records are selling well. But it is also possible to make a response based on an inaccurate perception of sales or a desire to stimulate sales of certain records. Second, the mechanism measures only the preference of a segment of XXX's audience; those who buy records and tapes. It is likely that there are many people who listen to the station and never or rarely make such purchases. Third, the selection of music is restricted. XXX asks for sales only on records it is already playing, not sales of Latino music in general. It is possible that records may be selling well that are not on the station's playlists. Fourth, the sampling is limited. The station calls only four stores a week and calls only stores specializing in Latino music. This excludes purchases of music in other outlets featuring Latino music.

In summation, the three formal audience feedback mechanisms used by XXX provide information which the station feels is useful to its smooth operation. But it is information which is defined by its utility to the station and its advertisers, not the needs of the audience to express itself. The measures are also basically indicators of consumption; consumption of the station's programming, consumption of products advertised on the station, and consumption of records played on the station through purchases. Thus, the formal audience feedback mechanisms can be described as extensions of the needs of the station and its desire to define its audience in certain terms, rather than an extension of the audience and its desire to express its feelings to the station.

Informal Feedback Mechanism. Informal audience feedback loops are, by their nature, difficult to describe and assess. They are also less integrated into the regular decision-making process of the station management. Often these avenues for audience input are more illusory than real: For instance, in interviews disc jockeys often mentioned that listeners would call them while they're on the air and ask that certain songs be played. However, the audience can only ask for songs that are on the weekly playlist and a disc jockey cannot replay a song until all songs on the playlist have been aired.

The basic means of informal feedback observed at the station include phone calls to the station, letters to the station, and meetings requested by community groups. The management expressed great interest in learning the views of listeners expressed in these ways and said the information was gathered and analyzed by different XXX staff members as they received it. If decisions are made they are made after the information has been analyzed and appropriate staff members consulted.

Two instances of changes that could have been based on informal audience feedback were observed at the station. It is not known how many other such changes were made or what other suggestions may have been made and not acted upon. One change involved the "loosening" of XXX's format to include the playlist of 10 *recuerdos* each week. According to the station management, listeners complained to the station about the constant rotation of the same 50 songs over and over each week. Thus, the station reacted by increasing its weekly playlist to 60 records and adding 10 additional songs from previous lists.

The second change involved the classification of groups on XXX's weekly playlists. The station was approached by local Latino musical groups and their supporters who wished to hear more locally-produced music on the station. Although the station did not make a specific commitment to play more local music the program director did begin to note the number of local groups on each week's playlist.

Although it is difficult to assess the influence of informal audience feedback, it is apparent that XXX's listeners do care about what they hear on the station and do make their views known to the management. In at least two instances these expressions of concern over a period of time did result in a change in station policy. Whether the changes implemented by the station fully addresses the concerns of the audience is not known. But it is apparent that the station management cares enough about listener input to reconsider at least some of its policies.

Discussion of Findings

The findings of this case study of one Spanish-language radio station should be read with some cautions in mind. First, the data and information generated through a case study of one Spanish-language radio station should not be applied or generalized to other stations. Second, the data and information on XXX accurately describe that station as it was operating in the mid-1970s. Since radio stations are not static institutions it is expected that some of these characteristics will change over time. Third, the data and information generated in the case study should be evaluated in the context of the survey data and comparative data in other chapters in this book to gain a more complete understanding of the operation of Spanish-language radio in the Southwest.

The findings of each section of the case study are presented at the end of each section. With these summaries in mind we can turn to an analysis of these individual findings.

The historical background on the station describes how the transition from part time to full time Spanish-language station was accompanied by an increased participation by management in the operation of Spanish-language programming and its economic rewards. It was also accompanied by an increased commercialization of time as measured by spot announcements and percentage of time sold commercially. Advertisers were charged more and the station increased in economic value. Thus, the change to primary Spanish-language programming was part of an overall plan to increase the value of the station economically to its Anglo owners.

At the same time the changeover witnessed a dislocation of the Spanish-language programmers from private entrepreneurs in business for themselves to employees of the station. It also saw a sharp increase in the percentage of entertainment programming and a resulting reduction of religious, informational, and discussion programs. While the percentage of entertainment programming continued to stay above 85% through the mid-1970s, the addition of regular newscasts in the early 1960s did add slightly to the amount of information carried by the station. However, a bilingual XXX listener who had clung to the station during the transition would find less variety and diversity in the station's programming in the 1970s than in the 1950s.

Later changes included the separation of the former brokers from the station, an increased emphasis on securing national advertising, and introduction of a tight Top 40 programming format. As a result the station replicated many of its English-language counterparts by building audience based on loyalty to the station's format sound, rather than the disc jockeys on the station.

The ownership and top management of the station is Anglo, but there is greater integration of Latinos in heading station departments than was found in the national survey discussed in Chapter 2. It was found that most of these Latinos are hired with previous experience in broadcasting in Latin America, rather than from the local Latino labor force. However, the management indicated a desire to hire more local Chicanos at the station and had made a conscious effort to do so in the most recent hires. Women were found as full time employees only in the office staffs of the station and had no regular time slots on the air or in sales or engineering.

The discussion of the station's economics, while limited in terms of specific figures, showed how the flow of economic resources to the station was dependent on the station's ability to sell its audience as a consumer market to advertisers. As a result of this, the station's programming format, including news and public service programming, had been designed to conform with the Top 40 format the station hoped would attract listeners between the ages of 18 and 49. Through a number of sales devices the station attempted to convince advertisers of the importance of the Latino audience, the ability of the station to reach that audience, and the cost effectiveness of XXX advertising. It was shown that the station is primarily dependent on retail outlets for its advertising and has drawn increasing percentages of its advertising from accounts handled by advertising agencies.

The station's programming was found to be an outgrowth of the economic concern for attracting a saleable audience. Thus, the entertainment programming, which comprised over 85% of the station's time, was a tightly packaged combination of music and recorded announcements with minimal talk from the disc jockeys. This format was selected because it was felt it would attract the 18–49 listeners desired by advertising agencies. Similarly, news and public service programming, which comprised less than 15% of the programming, were found to be tightly packaged around the Top 40 format and designed to make the least disruption in the entertainment programming. The sources for the largest percentage of music and the majority of news was found to be from outside the country. Thus, the station was in many ways an extension of Latin American music and news into the Chicano community. Public affairs programs, while affording some access to local community groups, were found to be scheduled at times when the audience was smallest.

The station's audience was found to be highly concentrated in the 18 to 49 age group desired by advertising agencies and quite large when compared with other English and Spanish-language radio stations in the area. It was also found to be an audience concentrated in lower income and socio-economic categories. An analysis of audience participation winners revealed a significant concentration in the lowest Latino median income residential areas and a significant lack of representation in moderate or upper income Latino districts. A comparison of XXX and English-language radio listeners in a low income district revealed XXX listeners to be older, less likely to be working, more dependent on Spanish, newer to the area, and more likely to prefer the term Mexicano than those listening to English-language radio.

The station's audience feedback loops were found to be primarily measures of consumption which provided specific types of information needed by the station, not a full reflection of what the audience felt about the station. Although it was also found that informal feedback channels had some influence on station decisions, it could not be determined if the station's reaction fully addressed the concerns of the audience or if other feedback to the station had not been dealt with.

Thus, the story of radio station XXX is the story of a station that grew from part time to full time Spanish-language programming. While this transition was taking place the locus of business moved away from the immediate community that comprised its audience and became a product of larger economic concerns. The change also witnessed the transition from listenership based on loyalty to a personality to listenership based on loyalty to the station. Once the station loyalty could be established through a standardization of the music and format the station could sell the audience as a more attractive commodity to larger advertisers. Thus, the station sought feedback from the audience which would reinforce its ability to attract and sell the audience desired by advertising agencies.

The story of Spanish-language ratio station XXX is the story of many radio stations in this country, particularly those in large metropolitan areas. It is hoped that this case study has illustrated how this process has affected one Spanish-langauge station. It is also hoped that others will study other stations to determine how they have evolved and what effect this has had on their service to their audience and community.

CHAPTER VI

Conclusions

This chapter presents the conclusions to the study of Spanish-language radio presented in this monograph, and uses the empirical evidence generated in the study to examine a theoretical framework which has been previously applied to the study of Chicano institutions in the United States. The chapter is divided into three sections. Section one presents the results of the study as they apply to the broader theoretical framework. Section two discusses the strengths and weaknesses of the study and makes recommendations for future research. Section three presents three policy recommendations for changes in the media industry based on this study.

Analysis of the Results of the Study

The results of the study were summarized at the end of each of the major sections: the census of Spanish-language radio in the United States and the Southwest, the comparative case studies of two San Antonio radio stations, and the case study of station XXX. It is not the purpose of this section to merely restate those results. Instead, it is felt that the reader and topic would be better served by an analysis of those results in the context of a broader theoretical analysis. Thus, the evidence from the study can be used to test the applicability of the broader framework to Spanish-language radio. At the same time the theoretical framework, if applicable, can add to our understanding of the role of Spanish-language radio in the development of the Chicano community.

Chicano Internal Colonialism. The framework that has been selected for testing is internal colonialism, a theoretical approach to the study of Chicanos that has been widely discussed by scholars in the 1970s.[1] The rationales for applying internal colonial theory has been amply discussed by other scholars with a firm background in theory and race relations.[2]

101

It is not our purpose to repeat the rationales here, although we do recommend them to those interested in the field. Instead, we propose to outline the basic characteristics of an internally colonized society and its communication systems, and then examine the previously discussed characteristics of Spanish-language radio to see if they conform to that framework.

Briefly, internal colonialism is a situation of inequality existing between two groups of people living in the same political, economic or geographic setting (such as a nation). The groups are usually distinguished from each other by racial, cultural, or linguistic differences. Internal colonialism is also characterized by elaborate social, political, and economic structures by which the dominant group exerts control over the subordinate group. This control often takes two forms. In one form the controlling group exploits the resources of the subordinate group and in a second form the subordinate group is dependent on the controlling group for other types of resources. Thus, exploitation and dependency are two critical mechanisms for the internally colonial apparatus to operate. Through these conditions and the operation of the colonial apparatus, the unequal distribution of resources continues in a manner which allows the dominant group to continue its control and prohibits the subordinate group from overcoming that control through existing channels.[3]

Communication media do not operate as an isolate in colonized settings. In fact, they often play a critical role in cultivating a collective consciousness that makes people receptive to the roles and responsibilities they are expected to assume. Media directed to internal colonies often serve to link those colonies with the dominant sectors in a manner favorable to the dominant group. Examination of communication media in colonized settings indicates communication systems are usually characterized by links to the dominant groups, serve to penetrate the internal colony for the dominant group or other outside interests, and have little or no audience input and feedback.[4]

Given the context of internal colonialism and the characteristics of media in colonized societies, it is possible to reexamine the operation of Spanish-language radio. A summary of the major findings of this study indicate how Spanish-language radio may be perpetuating the unequal, and internally colonial, relationships between Anglos and Chicanos in the United States.

National Census. The national survey established that the distribution of Spanish-language stations approximated the geographic distribution

102

of Latinos in the United States, thus linking the communication medium with the segment of the population that has been identified as a possible internal colony. The technical characteristics showed PSLR stations as only commercial operations, thus denying Chicanos access to educational PSLR stations in a manner similar to other forms of educational inequality between Anglos and Chicanos. The technical characteristics showed a significant difference betwen PSLR and SSLR stations, with those programming the most Spanish having more restrictions on broadcast hours and service class. Thus, it is apparent that the less desirable broadcast facilities are those devoting the most time to Spanish-programming. The network linkages were found to serve primarily for the advertising penetration of the Chicano community from the dominant economic sectors in order to stimulate purchases which would ultimately cause money to flow out of the Chicano community. No programming or news networks were found, as exist in English-language radio. The programming data showed that almost 90% of the stations offer Spanish only a few hours a week, thus denying their audience service most of the time, and that Spanish-language programming is a secondary format on most stations. The employment characteristics described a near classic colonial situation in which ownership, top management, and management of departments not requiring Spanish were largely held by Anglos. Latinos were found concentrated in management positions requiring use of Spanish or contact with the Chicano audience. Thus, the national data describe a communication system which addresses the internal colony, does not enjoy comparable characteristics with the system addressing the dominant group, and is controlled by dominant group members.

Southwestern Census. The census of Southwestern PSLR stations provided even more evidence supportive of the Chicano internal colonial analogy. For instance, ownership of PSLR is clearly dominated by Anglos. Anglo owners own more PSLR stations than their Spanish surnamed counterparts and also own more stations in wealthier markets. Conversely, PSLR stations owned by Spanish surnamed individuals were mostly confined to the poorer rural areas of the Southwest.

In terms of total assets and advertising rates, Anglo owners control stations with the highest total assets and advertising rates. Moreover, a few Anglo owners controlled more wealth, in terms of total assets, than the rest of the owners (both Anglo and Spanish surnamed) combined. Not a single Spanish surnamed owner was found among the stations falling in the categories with the highest advertising rates.

The same forms of differential levels of information available to each audience, that are observed in the content analysis of news programming, are also noted in the examination of PSAs. Whatever information is being transmitted through the PSAs of each station, it is clear that the Spanish speaking audience of KCOR is less able to use the PSA channel as a community voice than the English speaking audience of KONO. Though it is not contended here that these PSA patterns are a clear indication of Anglo domination of PSLR, these patterns do contribute further evidence of the lack of influence of the Chicano community over PSLR.

Case Study of XXX. The case study of radio station XXX, was highly descriptive but, nonetheless, provided information supportive of the internal colonialism analysis of unequal distribution of resources between colonizer and colonized. The history of the station showed how local Chicano entrepreneurs were dislocated and replaced as Spanish-language programming became more profitable for the Anglo station owners and management. At the same time, the increase of Spanish-language programming subjected the audience to greater commercialization and less diversity in programming than English-speaking listeners had been receiving. The ownership and management of the station is Anglo, with a greater integration of Latino managers than in the national or Southwestern surveys. However, employment of Latinos was found to favor those with previous experience in Latin American broadcasting, rather than local listeners from the Chicano community (although this had begun to change).

The information on economics and advertising illustrate how the station is able to sell a community that is weak economically as a viable consumer audience to what appear to be increasingly sophisticated advertisers. Thus, the utility of the station is as a vehicle to penetrate a largely low-income audience to extract its economic resources for advertisers. Programming was found to be largely entertainment with a heavy dependence on imported records. News and public affairs were secondary to the entertainment format. The station's audience was found to be in the most colonized sectors of the Chicano community, those with lowest incomes, limited use of English, least experience in the United States, and less likely to be employed. Formal feedback mechanisms illustrated the need of the station to tap the audience for certain measures of consumption, rather than the need for the audience to express itself to the station management, although in at least two instances informal audience feedback mechanisms did influence station decisions.

Summation. The analogy we draw from this evidence is not a rigid one. However, it is one which we feel supports the unequal distribution of resources inherent in the literature on internal colonialism. It also indicates that Spanish-language radio is reinforcing this unequal relationship between Anglo and Chicano communities, rather than breaking it down. The patterns of control and dependency in this situation are clear. We encourage others to develop their own analyses of Spanish-language radio and to submit other institutions affecting the Chicano community to similar scrutiny.

Analysis of the Study and Recommendation for Future Research

Use of the survey technique to gather data on PSLR stations was effective in that it utilized available information from public directories and station files. The fact that there is a single repository for station information made access to that information feasible, for the amount of effort employed, there was a large payoff in retrieved information. This would indicate that the use of survey techniques in the future would be profitable. However, there are limits to the type and amount of information available from previously gathered sources. Three research recommendations are made on the basis of the survey design.

First, there is a need for more information on PSLR related wealth. Although it was possible to measure the total assets of most stations, it was impossible to measure the worth of the individual owners, or of their additional properties. Both of these shortcomings limit the depth of inquiry that is possible on media generated wealth. Future studies should focus on determining the extent of PSLR, and PSLR related, wealth so as to provide a more complete picture of this aspect of the economic structure of the Chicano community. Present measures are limited to assessing what is in the public domain, and much of this already public information is quite spotty and incompletely reported; in part this is the fault of the repository agencies.

Second, we need to know more about the role of advertising in PSLR. Neither this study, nor previous studies, have adequately addressed the subject. Advertising is the core of commercial radio since it is the operational vehicle by which income actually enters the station. Information is present on the stations' advertising rates, but there is little information on advertising revenues, problems or practices. Advertising practices were discussed in the case study, but they were in the context of one station, and so revealed less about practices nationwide. There is also little information on whether advertisers affect station decisions and program content. A future study on the role played by PSLR sponsors in determining station policy and content would greatly contribute to our knowledge of PSLR operations and the role of PSLR as a community institution.

Third, more information is necessary on the mechanisms of control exercised by Anglos within the various PSLR stations. The indications of control and domination measured in this study invariably rely on measuring the effects of that control and domination. While this is generally satisfactory in gaining an initial understanding of PSLR control, it does not provide measures on how decisions are actually made, nor does it provide information on the roles played by the various participants. The assumptions made in this study on the behavior of Anglos and Chicanos affiliated with PSLR need to be examined within the organizational environment of the stations.

The Content Analyses

The content analysis of news programming provided a direct measure of the flow of information through both PELR and PSLR. The data gathered from the news broadcasts was easy to code and categorize. The analysis of the news also provided a measure, complementary to measures of wealth, thereby illustrating more than one form of inequality. Moreover, it provided a valuable comparison between English and Spanish language radio.

The content analysis also showed some important weaknesses as a technique. Primarily, it suffered from being difficult to apply outside of a case study format, thus, carrying with it the shortcomings of the case study approach, primarily that of generalizability. In addition, the technical limitation of conducting a content analysis of news broadcasts was such that it would be difficult to extent it beyond the case study level. The content analysis demanded a great deal of effort for limited gains. It took nearly as much time to gather the information from the content analysis, as it did to gather the information from the preliminary survey of PSLR stations. Thus, the content analysis was less cost effective than the PSLR station survey. Two research recommendations are made in light of the content analysis of news broadcasts.

First, more research is needed on the conduct of news operations within the stations. The content analysis of news provided information on the finished product of news broadcasting, but did not provide information on how the news is gathered, edited, or combined. Future research should focus on news operations within the organization, taking into account the unique constraints under which PSLR operates. Furthermore, because the question of information control has been raised in this study, it is recommended that future research into the internal operations of news broadcasting investigate the possibility of information control.

Second, there is a great need for research on the effects of news information. It is assumed in this study that information from news broadcasts is useful in making decisions about civic participation. This may not be the case. Future research should focus on the uses of broadcast news by English and Spanish speaking audiences. The possibility of different uses of the same bit of information, by each cultural group, should be investigated in order to determine if there is news information that is of greater or lesser value to each community. Future researchers should investigate the importance of broadcast news among the various information sources available to the Chicano community, as well as the effects of the information gap highlighted in this study.

The final research design used in this portion of the study was a content analysis of Public Service Announcements on one PELR and one PSLR station. Since this content analysis was also a case study, it was subject to the limitations inherent in both content analyses and case studies. The PSA content analysis provided information on the identities of PSA sponsors, and therefore, allowed the researcher to identify the community sectors in which the sponsors were located. As with the analysis of news broadcasts, the information on PSAs is preliminary information. Two recommendations are made on the basis of this content analysis.

First, there is a need for more information on noncommercial sponsor behavior. At present, there is little understanding of the sponsor's perceived gains, or of the sponsors' motivations for placing PSAs. This type of information will contribute to our understanding of the uses of PSLR by those who support it. This is particularly important since the data presented in this study have illustrated that there are two significantly different patterns of PSA sponsorship in PELR and PSLR.

Finally more information on the audience effects of PSAs is vitally needed. It is assumed in this study that PSAs act as an information channel to the Spanish speaking and English speaking listener; but we don't really know whether this is so. It is, therefore, important to ascertain whether this, in fact, is true; and if so, what is the utility of the information. A better understanding of the effects of PSA messages would potentially contribute to better access on the part of the Chicano community.

107

The In Depth Case Study

The case study of PSLR station XXX provided a look into ownership, employment, and operational patterns and practices. This was a significant approach in that it provided a rare glance into the total operations and practices of one large PSLR station in a lucrative market. Much of the quantitative data and inferences drawn from the survey and content analyses was effectively supplemented by the qualitative information in chapter V.

Although the information gathered from the case study was detailed and thorough, it presented a very time consuming process for the investigators. The same problems of cost and time effectiveness raised in the content analyses, were also raised in the case study. In addition, problems of setting up interviews and accessing the subjects in this personal form of analysis were considerable. Whatever the limitations, the payoff was great in that it provided an unprecedented view of the actual mechanisms of ownership and operations. Two recommendations for future research are made on the basis of the XXX study.

First, continued research focusing on the qualitative aspects of ownership and station operation is necessary. Although of considerable difficulty, this form of investigation produces a level of information currently lacking in examinations of broadcasting practices. In addition, it contributes to policy by providing new insights in areas of critical regulation.

Second, more research is needed on the internal mechanics of institutional racism. In several instances, employees at XXX discussed problems relating to Latinos working within a predominantly Anglo decision making structure. Although patterns of differential personnel distribution within organizations are readily identifiable, the experiences of individuals and groups of individuals within the organization are less easily identified. The case study approach, with its capacity for intense investigation, is particularly suitable to the gathering of this type of information. Only additional case studies focusing on aspects of institutional racism, however, will provide the generalizability that is lacking here.

Policy Recommendations

Three policy recommendations are directed at the relationship between the FCC and PSLR. Since broadcasting, as a federally regulated industry, is subject to changes in its operations due to federal requirements, it is important to focus on the role of the FCC in the determination of responsible broadcasting.

First greater station accountability should be a primary issue of regulatory consideration. These studies have demonstrated that in the areas of ownership, employment, and public service announcements, the Chicano community has limited access to the only broadcast medium widely broadcasting in Spanish. Additionally, the data indicate that limited access is not the same for all communities; indeed, the Anglo community appears to have greater access to English language radio than the Chicano community has to Spanish language radio. The twin regulatory issues of employment and ascertainment deserve special FCC attention as operational measures of Spanish language radio accountability.

Second, the accessibility and utility of public information deposited with the FCC presents a problem. In other words, there is a need for greater self-regulation on the part of the commission. The lack of consistent station data, and the commission's archaic filing system, created serious difficulties in the research for these studies. Data in the station files was neither standardized, nor complete; all categories had missing data where, theoretically, there should have been none. In examining the quality of information present in the files, it was apparent that FCC enforcement was either lax or non existent. Such low quality raw data makes it difficult for the researcher to conduct systematic investigations into nearly all aspects of broadcasting; FCC station information is simply not useful to the public in its current state of disarray, and so is "public information" only in the technical sense.

The final recommendation is for regulatory attention to those aspects of PSLR that contribute to its unique problems. In a sense, PSLR suffers from problematic influences that are exogenous. Ownership and employment patterns, as well as the information gap issue, have their seeds in the development and conduct of American broadcasting in general, rather than in the particulars of Spanish language broadcasting. Those factors which appear to function in English language broadcasting, such as absentee ownership of broadcast properties, an entrepreneurial philosophy toward multi station acquisitions, and free choice among many messages, are less clearly successful in PSLR. Because most PSLR stations are one of few (if not the only) sources of information in their communities, their ownership, employment and content characteristics place a burden on PSLR that is not felt on PELR. Certainly this burden is unfair, though unavoidable.

It is not clear that additional regulations will necessarily bring positive change to PSLR. Nor is it clear that changes should be expected from the industry which has operated with carte blanche for so many years. Public activism has shown itself to be neither consistent nor conclusively successful in efforts to change the practices of broadcasting. Of the three vehicles for reform in broadcasting, the commission appears to hold the greatest potential for working out a compromise that encourages the continued development of PSLR and reduces the media isolation that most Spanish speaking Americans live with.

Spanish language radio contains both a promise and a peril. It holds the promise of reducing the information gap and of using its influence in support of the equalization of relationships between the two communities. But it also holds a peril in contributing to the maintainance of information resources in the hands of the Anglo community. The future of successful relationships, and changes in structures, between the two communities depends, in part, on greater Chicano community access to the medium that broadcasts to it, and on greater Anglo community recognition of the special needs of the Spanish speaking community.

NOTES

[1]For general treatments of internal colonialism see Dale Johnson, "On Oppressed Classes," in James P. Cockcraft, Andre Gunder Frank and Dale Johnson, *Dependency and Underdevelopment* (Garden City, New York: Anchor Books, 1972), pp. 269–301, Pablo González-Casanova, *Democracy in Mexico* (London: Oxford University Press, 1970), pp. 71–103, and Pablo González-Casanova, "Internal Colonialism in National Development," in Irving Louis Horowitz, Josue de Castro and John Gerassi, *Latin American Radicalism* (New York: Vintage Books, 1969, pp. 61–74.

[2]For articles relating internal colonialism to Chicanos see Robert Blauner *Racial Oppression in America* (New York: Harper & Row, 1972), pp. 19–42; Rodolfo Acuña, *Occupied America: The Chicano's Struggle Toward Liberation* (San Francisco: Canfield Press, 1973), pp. 19–33, 123–146; Tomás Almaguer, "Toward the Study of Chicano Colonialism," *Aztlán*, Spring 1971, pp. 7–10; Mario Barrera, Carlos Muñoz, and Charles Ornelas, "The Barrio as an Internal Colony," in Harlan Hahn, *People and Politics in Urban Society* (Beverly Hills-London: Sage Publications, 1972), pp. 467–476; Guillermo Flores and Ronald Bailey, "Internal Colonialism and Racial Minorities in the U.S.: An Overview," in Frank Bonilla and Robert Girling, *Structures of Dependency* (United States of America: Frank Bonilla and Robert Girling, 1973), pp. 161–188; Guillermo Flores, "Race and Culture in the Internal Colony: Keeping the Chicano in his Place, in Bonilla and Girling, op cit., pp. 180–223; and Joan Moore, "Colonialism" The Case of the Mexican Americans, *Social Problems*, Spring 1970. For critiques of the applicability of internal colonial-

110

ism to Chicanos see Fred A. Cervantes, "Chicanos as a Post Colonial Minority: Some Questions Concerning the Adequacy of the Paradigm of Internal Colonialism," *Perspectivas en Chicano Studies* (Los Angeles: UCLA Chicano Studies Center, 1977), pp. 123–136 and Gilbert G. Gonzalez, "A Critique of the Internal Colony Model," *Latin American Perspectives*, Spring 1974.

[3]For a more complete operational definition of Chicano internal colonialism as applied in this study see Jorge Reina Schement, "Primary Spanish-language Radio as a Function of Internal Colonialism: Patterns of Ownership and Control," Ph.D. Dissertation, Stanford University, 1976, pp. 11–31.

[4]For a more complete exposition on the criteria for examining communication media in the colonial setting see Félix F. Gutiérrez, "Spanish-language Radio and Chicano Internal Colonialism," Ph.D. Dissertation, Stanford University, 1976, pp. 26–36.

APPENDICES

APPENDIX A

National Census of Spanish-language Radio Stations

Sources of Information

Sources of information used to gather the information on the national survey of Spanish-language radio were the 1974 *Broadcasting Yearbook* and the October 1, 1973 edition of *Spot Radio*. These are both sources of regularly updated public information on radio broadcasting in the United States. The specific editions were selected because they were the most recent available at the time research began and represent information in both publications gathered in the same time period.

The *Yearbook* was the basic source of information for much of what was analyzed in this section. Its Section B, "The Facilities of Radio," provided most of the descriptive information on the stations analyzed. The "Directory of AM and FM Radio Stations in the U.S." pp. B-3 through B-238, provided most of the information needed. When incomplete information was encountered in this section, the sections of "AM Station Call Letters," pp. B-250 through B-259; "Commercial and Educational FM Call Letters," pp. B-259 through B-266; "U.S. AM Radio by Frequencies," B-266 through B-287; "Table of FM Assignments," pp. B-290 through B-294; and "U.S. FM Radio by Frequencies and Channels," pp. B-298 through B-305 were consulted for the needed information. *Spot Radio* was utilized as a source of information on the radio stations only where incomplete or unclear information was provided in the *Yearbook* and as the source of information on the location of radio stations by Standard Metropolitan Statistical Area (SMSA).

Coding of the Information

Information was coded from the sources of information noted on to IBM FORTRAN Coding Forms according to a coding instruction sheet developed by Nicholas Valenzuela. Valenzuela, the author of several studies in Chicano communication research involving extensive computer analysis of information, was brought into the project to design the instructional sheet for coding the information from the sources to the IBM FORTRAN Coding Forms and coordinate most of the computer processing of the information. His responsibilities included refining the variables previously designated as relevant to the study so they would lend themselves to computer analysis, devising the methods for coding and verifying the information, and supervising computer analysis of the data. James Fleming, academic applications consultant at the California State University, Northridge Computer Center, also assisted in the computer analysis of the data.

115

An initial scheme for coding the information was designed and pretested on a sample of 25 radio stations. After the 25 stations had been coded the original scheme was analyzed and revised for greater efficiency and accuracy. A final coding scheme was developed and the information on the 485 radio stations transferred from the sources of information to the coding sheet. The coding of this information was conducted jointly by the principal investigator reading the information and Valenzuela coding it on the form. After the information was coded on the forms the data was transferred to computer cards by a professional key puncher employed by the Computer Center at California State University, Northridge.

Verification of Data

The data were verified by several systematic methods to insure the accuracy of information analyzed by statistical means. First, the key puncher sight verified the punched cards for columnar accuracy. Second, frequency tabulations were run for each variable and checked to verify that only values designated for that variable were coded. Third, cross-tabulations were run on mutually descriptive variables. These included crosstabulating the AM or FM variable with frequency, since an AM or FM station should always show a frequency within the AM or FM spectrum. The variable designating whether a station was primarily or secondarily Spanish was crosstabulated with the hours of Spanish programming, since the number of hours would indicate the emphasis on the language. The variable designating day or night operation was crosstabulated with day and night power, since day only stations would show no power at night. The stations' service class as granted by the FCC was also crosstabulated by AM and FM, since class assignments for the two frequencies are different. Class was also crosstabulated with whether stations were commercial or non-commercial for the same reason. The number or other special programs broadcast by the stations was crosstabulated by the number of hours of such programs, since there should be an equivalency in several cells of both crosstabulations. Format was crosstabulated with whether a station was primarily or secondarily Spanish, since stations with a Spanish format should be listed as primarily Spanish.

In each of these frequency runs and crosstabulations errors were checked with the original sources of information and corrected on the cards. Errors located in each of these frequency runs and crosstabulations were checked with the original sources of information and corrected on the computer cards. In each case other similarly situated stations were checked at random to determine whether or not the variable had been coded correctly. In each case errors were determined to be random and unsystematic.

Analysis of the Data

The data were batch processed by the Statistical Package for the Social Sciences (SPSS) Version of March 13, 1971 on the Control Data Corporation 3170 computers at California State University, Northridge.

In most cases variables were analyzed by a frequency distribution to show the characteristics of all stations broadcasting Spanish-language programs for that variable. There was interest in determining the characteristics of Spanish-language stations in relation to other stations. However, since there was no set of comparable information for all stations in the United States it was decided to compare the characteristics of stations which were primarily Spanish (half or more of their programs in Spanish) with stations which were secondarily Spanish (less than half of their programs in Spanish). Thus, most variables are also crosstabulated by the variable Primary or Secondary Spanish. In cases where national data on all radio stations was available it was included as a separate crosstabulation and the source noted. In order to determine the statistical significance of differences between stations in the separate categories the Chi Square test for Independence of Cells was applied. Differences reported as significant to the .10 level or higher were noted as significant.

Survey of PSLR Stations in the Southwest

Operational Definitions

1. Primary Spanish Language Radio

PSLR is any radio station broadcasting 50% or more of its total time in Spanish. The 50% figure was chosen for two reasons. First, use of percentage of time was a simple and straightforward way of identifying a station as primary or secondary Spanish language radio since each station publishes the amount of time devoted to each of its formats. Second, the fifty percent majority category was used because it was felt that stations which broadcast the majority of their time in Spanish would have more in common with each other, and comprise the group primarily listened to by most of the Chicano audience.

There was one drawback with the 50% decision. The problem was a lack of any comprehensive listing of PSLRs. A list of PSLRs in the Southwest was identified from those stations which identified their format as "Spanish", "Ethnic", or "Foreign" in the December 1, 1974 issue of *Spot Radio Rates and Data*. The list was rechecked with the individual station records filed with the FCC in Washington, D.C., and a list of 41 PSLR stations in the Southwest was compiled.[1]

2. The Census of 1970

The 1970 census was used as a source of population figures for the Chicano audience because it provides a widely accepted data set, useful information, and consistent measures.

There are also some problems created by using the census. First of all, much of the census data relies on the Spanish surname population. The use of this criterion tends to undercount the number of Chicanos in the population since it ignores those Chicanos without Spanish surnames.[2]

Further, the census tends to undercount Chicanos by failing adequately to count illegal Mexican aliens. This group forms an important part of the Spanish speaking audience. The constant influx of illegal Mexican aliens tends to reinforce the Spanish language as a repository for cultural values.[3] Although one recognizes the problems in using the census as a measure of population, the census is still the best available measure at this time.

3. The Southwest

The Southwest is composed of the five states of Arizona, California, Colorado, New Mexico and Texas. The census provides relatively complete information on Chicanos living in this section of the United States, but has very little information on Chicanos living outside of this area. Any survey of all of the PSLR stations in the U.S. would inevitably have included Puerto Rican and Cuban stations, and thus, would have made it difficult to isolate Chicano oriented stations.

Research Design

A survey was conducted of all (41) PSLR stations in the five Southwestern states. The call letters of the stations were drawn from the *1975 Broadcast Yearbook* and the December 1, 1974 issue of *Spot Radio Rates and Data*.[4]

Data was collected from the FCC station files on:
1) total assets;
2) advertising rate;
3) name or owner;
4) ethnic identity of owner;
5) percent of management with Spanish surnames;
6) ethnic identity of engineer;
7) percent of employees with Spanish surnames;
8) owner's additional properties;
9) name of market;
10) rank of market;
11) city of license;
12) state of license;
13) AM/FM;
14) type of license;
15) number of hours broadcast in Spanish.

The fact that all stations did not submit the same data, however, presented a major problem. Theoretically, every station submits the same required information to be filed with the FCC. In actual practice, this does not occur, particularly in the case of Spanish language stations with their traditional "poor relative" status within the FCC. Potential categories such as: liabilities; recent station income; employee income; owner income; management income; value of other properties held by the owner, were so poorly reported that they had to be dropped. What data has been gathered, and what categories have been included in this study, are generally complete.

NOTES

[1]*Spot Radio and Data*, Standard Rate and Data Service, Inc., Vol. 56, No. 12, December 1, 1974.

[2]For a more extensive discussion see:
"Counting the Forgotten:, A report of the U.S. Commission on Civil rights, Washington, D.C., April 1974, p. 72–75.

[3]Ellwyn R. Stoddard, *Mexican Americans*, Random House, New York, 1973, p. 115–118.

[4]*Spot Radio . . . , op. cit.*

APPENDIX C

Content Analysis Methodologies

Content Analysis of News Broadcasts

A news item was deemed "local news" if it made some specific reference to San Antonio or Bexar county in the story, although the words "San Antonio" or "Bexar county" were not specifically necessary; a news item with a direct reference to either the city or county was accepted.

By choosing the concept "local news", any decision about what might be "Chicano" or "Anglo" news was averted. It is evident that the Chicano and Anglo communities are not mutually exclusive. Therefore, many news items would have had relative applicability in both communities. Moreover, there was no way to determine whether a news item was of specific use to the Anglo or Chicano community.

A content analysis of KCOR and KONO news broadcasts was conducted using three news programs per day over a seven-day period for each station. Programs were taped at 9 and 10; 11 and 12; 3 and 4, English on the odd hours, Spanish on the even. (Technological limitations made it impossible to conduct simultaneous recordings.) Since neither station varied its news broadcasts on any set schedule, and since the news was different every day, it was not necessary to vary the time of taping.

Content Analysis of Public Service Announcements

The purpose of this content analysis was to determine the number of PSAs sponsored by "Chicano community organizations" on KCOR.

"PSAs" refer to those public messages that are broadcast at no cost to the sponsor, thus differentiating them from advertisements, which are paid for. "Chicano community" was defined as those census tracts in San Antonio with 51% or more Chicano population; likewise, "Anglo community" is defined as those census tracts with 51% or more Anglo population. A "Chicano community organization" was defined as an organization that has its headquarters geographically located in the Chicano community; an "Anglo community organization" is an organization that has its headquarters geographically located in the Anglo community.

A content analysis was taken of PSAs broadcast, during the past license period, by KCOR and KONO. Titles of each PSA, listed and filed with the station, were collected. The organizations sponsoring the PSAs were subsequently identified through the help of Jack Roth from KONO, Nathan Safir from KCOR, and Robert

121

Garza from the Mexican American Unity Council (MAUC). The organizations' addresses were then located in the telephone book. In addition, organizations listing the terms: "Chicano," "Latino," "Latin-American," "Mexican-American," "Raza," "Hispano," "Hispanic American" or "Spanish American" in their titles were classified as Chicano community organizations without references to their addresses. Using this method of classification, any organization sponsoring a PSA could be identified as either a "Chicano" or "Anglo" community organization.

The choice of "percent of residents in a census tract" as a category for distinguishing the Anglo from the Chicano community contained an inherent problem. Had San Antonio been a highly integrated city the use of census tracts to identify the two ethnic communities would have been unsuccessful. However, out of 212 census tracts only 47 (22%) had populations that were less than 75% of one ethnic group, and this was felt an acceptable figure. In the case of San Antonio, the level of segregation allowed the use of census tracts as identifiers.

APPENDIX D

XXX *Case Study Methodology*

The information which provides the basis for the case study of a Spanish-language radio station generated from radio station XXX. The station, a primary Spanish-language station, serves a metropolitan area in the Southwestern United States. In order to gain access to the station, its personnel and records, a written research proposal was made to the station management following preliminary interviews and discussions. This proposal outlined an eight-week research period in which eight aspects of the station operation would be investigated. The station management agreed to the research plan, agreed to allow access to certain station records, pledged the cooperation of the staff, and allowed the use of the station copying machine.

The actual research took place over a three and one-half month period in the mid-1970s. During this period the researcher visited the station each workday and followed the research schedule outlined in the proposal approved by management. The information and data generated were then analyzed in a preliminary review. The station was visited again for a period of 10 days following this analysis for additional information gathering.

The information generated in the case study was gathered with four different research techniques. These were:

Analysis of Documents. The station management facilitated access to documents on its operation. These included: past license renewal applications of the station, station logs, station playlists, public service announcement records, employment data, advertising promotional materials, and other records utilized in the station's operation. Specific documents and their use are discussed in relevant subsections of the chapter. Only documents or files to which access was specifically authorized were utilized in preparing the study.

Observation. Station employees in specific job categories were observed as they performed job related tasks. This included visiting clients with advertising salesmen, observing disc jockeys while they were on the air, observing the preparation of advertising spots, observing members of the news department, and observing other employees.

Interviewing. Station employees were also interviewed about their responsibilities and attitudes. Interviews were conducted with management personnel, account executives, disc jockeys, members of the news department, and other employees responsible for specific parts of the station's operation. All interviews were tape recorded and transcribed. Interviews were conducted in both Spanish and English.

123

Content Analysis. The station's programming content was analyzed through two samplings. One sampling was a composite week for an entire year. This sampling was based on a stratified random sample of seven days in that year. The sampling was stratified to be representative of periods of the week and seasons of the year. The material analyzed from this composite week is based on the station's program logs for the days selected. A second content analysis was based on recording of station broadcasts over a one-week period. This was also a stratified random sample. The sample was stratified to represent the different broadcast time periods recorded by the commercial rating services each broadcast day. Using random selection one half-hour period was selected out of each of the rating service time periods each day of the seven-day period and recorded.

Using these research techniques, plus additional interviews with former employees, information about the station was gathered in eight areas of concern that make up the subheadings of the case study chapter. These were: (1) development of the station, (2) management and employment, (3) economics, (4) entertainment programming, (5) news, (6) public service programming, (7) audience characteristics, and (8) audience feedback.

Readers of this study should be aware of the inherent limitations of a study of this type. One limitation is access to information. Since the station management controls access to records and other information sources a complete access to all types of information relevant to the study was not possible. A second limitation is the extent to which the findings in the case study can be generalized to other Spanish-language radio stations. Case studies are recognized as important research approaches because they allow the researcher to become intimately involved with a specific unit of analysis. However, an inherent limitation is that such information can be applied to other units (in this case other Spanish-language radio stations) only with the greatest caution. A third limitation is the time frame in which the information and data were gathered. Radio stations are not static institutions. They are, instead, in a constant stage of evolution and development. The information and analysis presented in this chapter is an accurate reflection of what was found at the station during the period in which information was gathered and analyzed. However, it is to be expected that certain elements in this analysis will change.

BIBLIOGRAPHY

GOVERNMENT DOCUMENTS

Johnson, Nicholas. "CATV: The New Frontier in Public Service Programming," *Public Notice.* Federal Communications Commission, Washington, D.C., June 17, 1971.

Johnson, Nicholas. "CATV: New Hope for the Minorities," *Public Notice.* Federal Communications Commission, Washington, D.C., June 26, 1973.

U.S. Commission on Civil Rights, *Counting the Forgotten: The 1970 Census Count of Persons of Spanish Speaking Background in the United States.* Washington, D.C., April 1974.

U.S. Commission on Civil Rights, *Mexican Americans and the Administration of Justice.* Washington, D.C., March 1970.

U.S. Commission on Civil Rights, *Mexican American Study Project, Reports I-VI.* Washington, D.C., 1972–1974.

U.S. Bureau of the Census, *Current Population Reports Series P-20*, Persons of Spanish Origin in the United States, November 1969. Washington, D.C., 1971.

U.S. Bureau of the Census, *Census of the Population: 1970 Subject Reports PC(2)-1D*, Persons of Spanish Surname. Washington, D.C., 1973.

U.S. Bureau of the Census, *Census of the Population: 1970 Subject Reports Final Report PC(2)-1C*, Persons of Spanish Origin. Washington, D.C., 1973.

U.S. Office of Censorship, *Code of Wartime Practices for American Broadcasters,* Washington, D.C. (specific editions: June 15, 1942; February 1, 1943; December 1, 1943; May 15, 1943).

BOOKS

Acuña, Rodolfo. *Occupied America: The Chicano's Struggle Toward Liberation.* (San Francisco: Canfield Press, 1972).

Allen, Robert. *Black Awakening in Capitalist America.* (Garden City: Anchor Books, 1970).

Blauner, Robert. *Racial Oppression in America.* (New York: Harper & Row, 1972).

de Rivera, Marta Colomina. *El Huésped Alienante.* (Maracaibo, Venezuela: Editorial Universitaria, 1968).

González-Casanova, Pablo. *Democracy in Mexico.* (London: Oxford University Press, 1970).

Grebler, Leo, Joan Moore and Ralph Guzman. *The Mexican American People.* (New York: The Free Press, 1970).

Head, Sydney. *Broadcasting in America.* (Boston: Houghton Mifflin Company, Inc., 1972).

Kotler, Philip. *Marketing Management.* (Englewood Cliffs: Prentice-Hall, Inc., 1972).

LaBrie, Henry G. *The Black Press in America: A Guide.* (Coralville: Mercer House Press, 1972).

Lamar, Howard Roberts. *The Far Southwest 1846–1912: A Territorial History.* (New York: W. W. Norton & Company, Inc., 1970).

Landry, Robert J. *This Fascinating Radio Business.* (New York: The Bobbs-Merrill Company, 1946).

Lerner, Daniel and Wilbur Schramm (eds.). *Communication and Change in Developing Countries.* (Honolulu: East-West Center Press, 1967).

Lewels, Francisco J. *The Uses of Media by the Chicano Movement.* (New York: Praeger Publishers, Inc., 1974).

Lichty, Lawrence and Malachi Topping. *American Broadcasting.* (New York: Hastings House, 1975).

Longman, Kenneth A. *Advertising.* (New York: Harcourt Brace Jovanovich, Inc., 1972).

Mattalart, Armand, Patricio Biedma and Santiago Funes. *Comunicación Masiva y Revolución Socialista.* (México: Editorial Diógenes, S.A., 1972).

Meinig, D. W. *Southwest.* (New York: Oxford University Press, 1971).

Menéndez, Antonio. *Comunicación Social y Desarrollo.* Facultad de Ciencias Políticas y Sociales, Serie Estudios 24. (México: Universidad Autónoma de México, 1972).

Morales, Armando. *Ando Sangrando: A Study of Mexican-American Police Conflict.* (La Puente: Perspectiva Publications, 1972).

Paredes, Américo. *With the Pistol in His Hand.* (Austin: University of Texas Press, 1971).

Pasquali, Antonio. *Comunicación y Cultura de Masas.* (Caracas, Venezuela: Monte Avila Editores, C.A., 1972).

Pitt, Leonard. *The Decline of the Californios.* (Berkeley: University of California Press, 1966).

Pye, Lucien (ed.). *Communication and Political Development.* (Princeton: Princeton University Press, 1963).

Pyle, William W. and John A. White. *Fundamental Accounting Principles.* (Homewood: Richard D. Irwin Press, 1966).

Rogers, Everett M. and F. Floyd Shoemaker. *Communication of Innovations.* (New York: The Free Press, 1971).

Schiller, Herbert I. *Mass Communications and American Empire.* (Boston: Beacon Press, 1971).

Schramm, Wilbur. *Mass Media and National Development.* (Stanford: Stanford University Press, 1964).

Shurick, E. P. J. *The First Quarter Century of American Broadcasting.* (Kansas City: Midland Publishing Company, 1946).

Silva, Ludovico. *Teoría y Práctica de la Ideología.* (México: Editorial Nuestro Tiempo, S.A. 1971).

Spot Radio. (Skokie: Standard Rate and Data Service, October 1, 1973).

Wells, Alan. *Picture-Tube Imperialism?* (Maryknoll: Orbis Books, 1972).

1974 Broadcasting Yearbook. (Washington, D.C.: Broadcasting Publications, Inc., 1974).

ARTICLES

Aguayo, Joseph. "Latinos: Los Que Importan Son Ustedes," *Sales & Marketing Management*, July 11, 1977.

Almaguer, Thomás. "Toward the Study of Chicano Colonialism," *Aztlan.* Spring 1971.

"America's Spanish Treasure," *Sponsor.* October 18, 1965.

Arciga, Pepe. "Influx from Mexico Boosts Movie Trade," *Los Angeles Times.* May 1, 1965, Part III, p. 8.

Armon, Glenn. "Minorities Market Ethnic Broadcasters Make an Effective Pitch," *Barrons*, September 3, 1973.

Arnheim, Rudolf and Martha Collins Bayne. "Foreign Language Broadcasting over Local American Stations," in Lazarsfeld, Paul and Frank N. Stanton. *Radio Research 1941.* (New York: Duell, Sloan and Pearce, 1941).

Auerbach, Alexander. "The Chicano Clout: Overlooked Market Packs Heavy Wallet," *Los Angeles Times.* September 3, 1972, Section E, pp. 1–3.

Bailey, Ronald. "Economic Aspects of the Black Internal Colony," in Bonilla, Frank and Robert Girling. *Structures of Dependency.* (United States of America: Frank Bonilla and Robert Girling, 1973).

Barrera, Mario, Carlos Muñoz and Charles Ornelas. "The Barrio as an Internal Colony," in Hahn, Harlan. (ed.). *People and Politics in Urban Society*, (Beverley Hills-London: Sage Publications, 1972).

"Brown is Richer than Black," *Sales Management.* December 31, 1971.

Cervantes, Fred A. "Chicanos as a Post Colonial Minority: Some Questions Concerning the Adequacy of the Paradigm of Internal Colonialism," *Perspectivas en Chicano Studies.* (Los Angeles: UCLA Chicano Studies Center, 1977).

Christian, Jane McNab and Chester C. Christian, Jr. "Spanish Language and Culture in the United States," in Fishman, Joshua. *Language Loyalty in the United States.* (The Hague: Mouton & Co., 1966).

Córdova, Antonio. "New Mexico: A Colony of the United States," *Tricontinental.* September 1972.

Depland, Herbert. "A Comparative Study in the License Renewal Applications of Black and White Owned Radio Stations," *Journalism Abstracts.* 1972.

Ferretti, Fred. "The White Captivity of Black Radio," in Wells, Alan (ed.). *Mass Media & Society.* (Palo Alto: National Press Books, 1972).

Flores, Guillermo. "Race and Culture in the Internal Colony: Keeping the Chicano in His Place," in Bonilla, Frank and Robert Girling (eds.). *Structures of Dependency.* (United States of America: Frank Bonilla and Robert Girling, 1973).

Flores, Guillermo and Ronald Bailey. "Internal Colonialism and Racial Minorities in the U.S.: An Overview," in Bonilla, Frank and Robert Girling, *Structures of Dependency* (United States of America: Frank Bonilla and Robert Girling, 1973).

"Foreign Language Radio to Clean Up," *Variety.* May 20, 1942.

"Foreign Stations 'Confess'," *Variety.* May 20, 1942.

Friedrich, Carl J. "Foreign Language Radio and the War," *Common Ground,* Autumn 1942.

Furtado, Celso. "U.S. Hegemony and the Future of Latin America," in Horowitz, Irving Louis, Josue de Castro and John Gerassi. *Latin American Radicalism*. (New York: Vintage Books, 1969).

González-Casanova, Pablo. "Internal Colonialism in National Development," in Horowitz, Irving Louis, Josue de Castro and John Gerassi. *Latin American Radicalism*. (New York: Vintage Books, 1969).

Gonzalez, Gilbert G. "A Critique of the Internal Colony Model," *Latin American Perspectives*. Spring 1974.

Graham, Robert Somerville. "Spanish-language Radio in Northern Colorado," *American Speech*. October 1962.

"Habla Usted Español?" *Media/Scope*. September 1968.

Hill, Donald K. "The Broadcasting Industry and Black Cultural Restitution," *The Review of Black Political Economy*. Autumn 1970.

"Hispanos Have Small Voice in Radio Broadcasting," *Denver Post*, December 23, 1972.

Jenks, Edward. "What Are They Saying?" *New York Times*, June 28, 1942.

Johnson, Dale. "On Oppressed Classes," in Cockroft, James D., Andre Gunder Frank, and Dale Johnson (eds.). *Dependency and Underdevelopment*. Garden City: Anchor Books, 1972).

"Latino Media: Available in Any Mood from Conservative to Salsa," *Sales & Marketing Management*, July 11, 1977.

Lucraft, Howard. "National Advertisers Woo Spanish-Language Market, Push Radio," *Advertising Age*. March 2, 1970.

Martinez, Richard and Gilbert Lopez. "Reapportionment Revisited 1960," *La Raza*. January 1972.

"Media Briefs," *Los Angeles Times*. July 6, 1975, Part VII, p. 5.

Morales, Armando. "The Collective Preconscious and Racism," *Social Casework*. May 1971.

Moore, Joan, "Colonialism: The Case of the Mexican Americans," *Social Problems*. Spring 1970.

O'Connor, Douglas and Gayla Cook. "Black Radio: The 'Soul' Sellout," *The Progressive*. August 1973.

"Public Access Groups Reaffirm Objectives," *Broadcasting*. June 23, 1973.

"Radio Report," *Television/Radio Age*. November 27, 1972.

Romano, Octavio. "The Anthropology and Sociology of the Mexican American: The Distortion of Mexican American History," *El Grito*. Fall 1968.

Ruiz, Antonio. "The National Latino Media Coalition at the NCTA Convention," *Cablelines*. July 1973.

Rustin, Dan. "The Spanish Market: Its Size, Income and Loyalties Make it a Rich Marketing Mine," *Television/Radio Age*. October 2, 1972.

Salazar, Rubén. "The Mexican American Newsbeat—Past Practices and New Concepts," in *Southwest Texas Conference on Mass Media and Mexican Americans*. Community Relations Service, U.S. Department of Justice, (San Antonio: St. Mary's University, January 1969).

Schement, Jorge Reina and Félix F. Gutiérrez with Oscar Gandy, Tim Haight and M. Esteban Soriano. "The Anatomy of a License Challenge," *Journal of Communication*. Winter 1977.

Schement, Jorge Reina. "Literature on the Chicano Audience in Review," *Aztlan*. Spring 1978.

Schement, Jorge Reina. "Who Owns Spanish Language Radio?," *Agenda*. September/October, 1977.

Schement, Jorge Reina and Ricardo Flores. "The Origins of Spanish-Language Radio: The Case of San Antonio, Texas," *Journalism History*. Summer 1977.

"So They All Speak Spanish," *Media Decisions. May* 1977.

"Spanish-Americans: Alike and Different," *Sales Management*. October 2, 1972.

"Spanish-language Market Study," *Television//Radio Age*. November 7, 1977.

"Spanish Market: Undersold, Undervalued," Special Report, *Broadcasting*. September 19, 1966.

"Spanish Program Firm," *Broadcasting*. June 15, 1939.

"Station Rankings to Shift in Ethnic-rating Storm?," *Television/Radio Age*. February 19, 1973.

"Strict Checks Not Needed for Non-English Programs," *Broadcasting*. March 19, 1973.

"Success Stories, Research Help Spanish Station Sales," *Television/Radio Age*. November 7, 1977.

Surlin, Stuart H. "Black-oriented Radio Programming to a Perceived Audience," *Journal of Broadcasting*. Summer 1972.

"Station Rankings to Shift in Ethnic-rating Storm?" *Television/Radio Age*. February 19, 1973.

Tebbel, John. "Newest TV Boom: Spanish-language Stations," *Saturday Review*. June 8, 1968.

"Those Spanish Language 11 Million," *Media Decisions*. March 1972.

Turner, Ralph H. and Samuel J. Surace. "Zootsuiters and Mexicans: Symbols in Crowd Behavior," *The American Journal of Sociology*. Vol. LXII, 1956.

Vaca, Nick. "The Mexican American in the Social Sciences, 1912–1970," *El Grito*. Spring and Summer 1970.

Warshauer, Mary Ellen. "Foreign Language Broadcasting," in Fishman, Joshua. *Language Loyalty in the United States*. (The Hague: Mouton & Co., 1966).

"Y&R Ethnic Unit: Finding and Reaching Minority Markets," *Broadcasting*. June 4, 1973.

REPORTS

Audience Estimates in the ARB Market of Los Angeles. (Beltsville, Maryand: American Research Bureau, April/May 1973).

Chicano Media Challenge: Basta Ya. Freedom of Information Center Publication No. 282. (Columbia, Missouri: University of Missouri School of Journalism, May 1972).

Dordick, H. S. and Nicholas A. Valenzuela. *A Study of Mexican American Information Sources and Media Usage in Boyle Heights (East Los Angeles)*. (Los Angeles: Annenberg School of Communications, University of Southern California, December 1974).

Garnett, Bernard. *How Soulful is "Soul Radio"?* (Nashville: Race Relations Information Center, 1970).

How Blacks and Spanish Listen to Radio Report 2, Arbiton Radio, January 1976.

129

Meyer, Anthony S. *Black Voices and Format Regulations: A Study in Black-oriented Radio.* (Stanford: ERIC Clearinghouse on Media and Technology, 1971).

Radio Stations in the United States Broadcasting Foreign Language Programs. (New York: American Council for Nationalities Service, 1970).

Rickard, Judy and Peggy England. *Media Habits of Mexican Americans and Other Minorities in Santa Clara County.* (San Jose: Institute for Business and Economic Research, California State University, San Jose, July 1973).

Surlin, Stuart H. *Ascertainment of Community Needs by Black-oriented Radio Stations.* (University of Georgia School of Journalism, January 1972).

The Role and Functions of Spanish-language-only Television in Los Angeles. Center for Urban and Regional Studies. (Claremont: The Claremont Graduate School, 1973).

Valenzuela, Nicholas. *Media Habits and Attitudes of Mexican Americans.* (Austin: Center for Communication Research, University of Texas, 1973).

Dissertations and Theses

Brennan, James Edward. "A Study of the Channels of Communication Used by *Spanish-Named Residents of San Antonio, Texas,*" Ph.D. Dissertation, Louisiana State University and Agricultural and Mechanical College, 1968.

Bundy, Miriam Jean Seger. "A Comparison of the English and Spanish Mass Media Preferences of Mexican Americans in East Los Angeles," Masters Thesis, California State University, Fullerton, 1973.

Cox, Dorrit Sue. "Spanish-Language Television in the United States: Its Audience and Its Potential," Master's Thesis, University of Illinois, 1969.

Gutiérrez, Félix F. "Spanish-language Radio and Chicano Internal Colonialism," Ph.D. Dissertation, Stanford University, 1976.

Meyers, Gail Eldridge. "A Study of the Channels of Communication Used by One-Hundred Spanish-Named of Denver, Colorado," Ph.D. Dissertation, University of Denver, 1959.

Schement, Jorge Reina. "Primary Spanish-language Radio As a Function of Internal Colonialism: Patterns of Ownership and Control," Ph.D. Dissertation, Stanford University, 1976.

Speeches and Presentations

Cervantes, F. A. "Chicanos as a Post Colonial Minority: Some Questions Concerning the Adequacy of the Paradigm of Internal Colonialism," Paper presented at the Annual Convention of the National Chicano Social Science Association, Austin, Texas, April 12, 1975.

Surlin, Stuart H. "Percentage of Air Time Devoted to News and Public Service Programming by Black-oriented Radio," Paper presented to the Minorities and Communication Division, Association for Education in Journalism, 1972.